'Hope is a consistent truth-sharer and an incredible advocate for young people. The courage she has in sharing her own story, and the boldness to proclaim the message of freedom throughout this book, are refreshing and always needed.'
Emma Borquaye, founder of Girl Got Faith

'A raw, thought-provoking and engaging book. Filled to the brim with important topics and conversations. With practical steps and moments of prayer throughout, this book truly does have Jesus at its centre.'
Tom Clark, Youth Director and HTB Livestream Pastor

'In this book, Hope vulnerably and honestly shares her story alongside her wrestles with mental health and faith. In it, she offers a theological basis for her insights and shares the wisdom of others who have also explored these topics of personal growth and faith in their own lives in some way. This book will draw you deeper into who you are and into faith in Jesus.'
The Revd Deborah Coyne, vicar in the Church of England

'With mental health concerns on the rise across the globe, Hope truly lives up to that name and message by providing readers a glimpse into her own life and story. I believe that, in her new book, *You are Free (Even If You Don't Feel like It)*, Hope shares with us readers some of the deepest and darkest moments of her life so that we can experience freedom through the power of vulnerability, our testimonies and our hope in Jesus. I recommend that anyone wanting to get a first-hand glimpse into the world of mental health be challenged by this story in order to help others. I pray that you are just as encouraged as I was upon reading!'
Myunique Inez, @instagramforbelievers

'Hope's powerful story will literally give hope to countless others that freedom and healing is possible when we are willing to allow God to do a deep work in our lives.'
Jane Kirby, *Truth Magazine*

'Having heard Hope speak, I knew what a brilliant communicator she is: authentic, real and passionate; and this brilliant book is the same. Using her story, the stories of others and biblical reflections, Hope tells it as it is. I am sure this book will be a lifeline to lots of people; it is raw, honest and deeply inspiring.
Patrick Regan OBE, Kintsugi Hope

'Hope shares her powerful story with such raw beauty. To read her book is to go on a journey, in what feels like a safe space, of confronting our pain and grasping how much God truly loves us and knows us. Woven in are useful practical tools rooted in Scripture, with testimonies from a whole range of people to learn from and relate to. Ultimately all of this feels like an invitation to say "yes" to living in the glorious freedom that God calls each of us to.'
Julia Strachan, Atlantic world-record rower, author and anti-slavery campaigner

'Hope's honesty about her own struggles with an eating disorder, mental health and faith is so refreshing and raw. We know as Christians that God doesn't promise us a life free from struggles; but when we feel trapped by shame or lies or fear, how can we ever be truly free? This book will help you to understand in a new, profound and practical way how unique, significant and loved by God you are, and how there is always a path, however narrow, to finding freedom.'
Simon Thomas, TV presenter

'Hope's gift is in speaking truth over the lies we commonly tell ourselves, without ever preaching or standing on her high horse. Her personal story and struggles bring authenticity and gentleness to this impactful book. *You Are Free (Even If You Don't Feel like It)* is the ideal companion for anyone who is on a journey to total freedom – and aren't we all? It's honest, moving and so very human.'

Lauren Windle, author, journalist and presenter

Hope Virgo is the author of *Stand Tall, Little Girl* (Trigger, 2019), and a multi-award-winning international leading advocate for people with eating disorders. Hope helps young people and employers, including schools, hospitals and businesses, to deal with the rising tide of mental health issues. She is also a recognized media spokesperson, having appeared on various programmes and platforms, including *BBC Newsnight*, *Victoria Derbyshire*, *Good Morning Britain*, Sky News and BBC News.

HOPE VIRGO

YOU ARE FREE

even if you don't feel like it

First published in Great Britain in 2022

Society for Promoting Christian Knowledge
36 Causton Street
London SW1P 4ST
www.spck.org.uk

British Library Cataloguing-in-Publication Data
A catalogue record for this book is available from the British Library

ISBN 978-0-281-08614-6
eBook ISBN 978-0-281-08615-3

1 3 5 7 9 10 8 6 4 2

Typeset by Fakenham Prepress Solutions, Fakenham, Norfolk NR21 8NL
First printed in Great Britain by Clays the Printer

eBook by Fakenham Prepress Solutions, Fakenham, Norfolk NR21 8NL

Produced on paper from sustainable sources

To my husband, family, godparents and friends,
and all those who have been with me in my battle and on my
journey,
helping me with patience, love and kindness,
and challenging me when I needed it.

And to those who feel as if life is like scaling a relentless mountain
at times:
I hope you find some peace through this book.
Your bravery in keeping going when things seem so hard is
inspiring.

Contents

Foreword

I don't know whether Hope's parents realized when they named her Jennifer 'Hope' Virgo how apt that name would be. Her life epitomizes 'hope' to so many people, and this book is all about hope.

I first met Hope in September 2019 when she came to Alpha and joined a small group with Nicky and me. She was absolutely delightful and we soon started to hear more of the story of her life – the challenges she had faced and how she had gone through some really difficult times.

Since then I have been amazed by what Hope has achieved as a spokesperson, working to raise awareness of the very difficult and complex issue of eating disorders. Hope has visited schools, businesses, churches – and even 10 Downing Street – to raise awareness of the complex issues surrounding this aspect of mental illness and mental health and well-being.

I have one friend who was in hospital suffering from a severe eating disorder, surrounded by others with similar conditions. Hope kindly went to visit my friend. When she entered the wing, they were all so excited to see her because she understands their struggles and is a radiant example of how she has overcome this serious illness. Hope has given her life to trying to make a difference to the many girls and boys, and women and men, who are struggling in this area.

I've met many wonderful people who've been battling with their relationship with food – often for years and in silence. It is absolutely heartbreaking. We've had people in our Alpha group who have been in recovery from issues to do with food. We also have congregation members who struggle, and I had a flatmate years ago with a serious eating disorder. I know for myself, particularly as a teenager, that my relationship with food was not healthy. Many people struggle so hard to get free from this horrible disease. I have seen how it consumes every area of their lives and robs them of all that is good.

The pressure on young people to look a certain way is huge. We have to look 'perfect'. The situation has got far worse in recent years. On social media we try to project a perfect version of ourselves – and every photograph is scrutinized. There seems to be no escape. People struggling with their relationship with food are getting younger and younger, causing endless pain to themselves and their families.

There is so much shame attached to eating disorders. That is why it is very brave of Hope to speak out and bring this issue into the open. There are also many aspects of her story that will speak to those suffering with their mental health and well-being generally, no matter how it presents itself in their day-to-day lives.

Hope helps to bring hope to people's lives, through helping people to take seriously the very real challenges of this aspect of mental illness.

People can recover from the grip of these eating disorders. Some people are healed dramatically, but for most people it requires time, hard work and perseverance. What the majority of people need most is supportive friends and family members, professional help and, most of all, the realization that we are all precious children of God, made in his beautiful image.

Hope is a hero. I fail to see how anyone reading this book could not benefit from it. If you are struggling with an eating disorder or poor mental health generally, then this book is a mine of wisdom, advice and hope. If you know someone who is struggling, this book will equip you to be someone who is better able to bring them hope.

Pippa Gumbel

Acknowledgements

A huge thank-you to Elizabeth Neep, and all those at SPCK Publishing. Thank you for taking a risk with me, for being patient and understanding, and for helping me to tell this story. Without you, the book would be unstructured and probably still lurking in my laptop!

A huge thank-you to all those who let me interview you and pick your brains for this book; without you it would not have been possible!

To Verity, Jemima, Sarah, Ruth, Lauren and Pippa, who grappled with all my questions on faith and mental health. For sitting up and talking to me in the early hours of the morning, and being on the end of WhatsApp when I had my rather random thought processes.

To Pippa and Nicky Gumbel, Jemima Haley and Stephen Foster, who were patient, kind and understanding as they led my Alpha Group.

To all my friends who have cheered me on through this whole process and kept me going. Thank you for believing in me and my recovery process.

To all those people who bravely shared their experiences of church life and its impact on their mental health, to those people who email me every day with snippets of their stories. It is these stories that inform so much of my research and my passion and keep me grounded.

Acknowledgements

To my family, who have supported me throughout my whole journey of recovery and who support me now in sharing my story even when it feels uncomfortable.

To my husband, for listening 24/7 to me talk about eating disorders and mental health and for letting me quote statistic after statistic on every lockdown walk. Thank you for putting up with the stress over book deadlines and campaign time frames!

Introduction

'God loves you so much' . . . 'You are created in God's image' . . . 'Love yourselves because God loves you' . . . The words echoed round the humid tent, touching the thousands of young people packed inside. I was at yet another Christian festival that I knew on some level held the power to change people's lives for ever – well, *other* people's lives, at least.

As I looked around the tent at people crying or starting to walk forward in response to the calls to prayer, I was already convincing myself that these words weren't meant for me. I sat there telling myself that if God really cared, he would make it so blatantly obvious that I was meant to walk forward to receive prayer. That if he *really* wanted to change my life, he would have someone say my name across the speakers.

But how could God really love me if he had left me alone for so long and caused me so much pain? If God really loved me, surely he would take all of it away in an instant? I didn't get it. And so I remained glued to the spot, fiddling with my hair, rearranging where it sat on my head, feeling hotter and more uncomfortable with every passing moment until I found myself wiping the sweat from my brow. I would just sit there for a few more minutes and see what happened, whether I started to feel anything other than discomfort . . . but nothing. Then again, why would God call my name while my life was such a mess?

I mouthed to my friend, who was sitting cross-legged on the floor just a few feet away, that I would catch her later, and stood up to walk past hundreds of people, all fully engaged, to slip out of the nearest exit. With every step away from the meeting tent I felt the tears starting to form, but I wasn't going to let them come. How could I? No one knew what was going on; no one would understand. My life felt like a mess. I was at a Christian festival where everyone seemed so close to God and yet I'd spent the last 24 hours chatting up guys and trapped in a cycle of calorie counting, self-hatred and shame. By the time I had got back to my church's campsite, I had managed to stow all my emotions tightly away. That was the way I liked it. And so I simply waited for my friends to come back to the tents for lunch, a lunch through which I would struggle and then rush to the toilets to throw up to get it out of my body.

As I sat there, waiting for my church group to arrive back from the festival's main meeting, I felt so alone, so trapped in my own thoughts. I honestly didn't feel good enough to be in the room with thousands of others responding to worship and ministry, never mind walking up to the stage for prayer. Little did I know then that, 15 years later, I would be responding to another 'altar call', giving my life back to God, and that one day I would be provided with a platform to share my experiences of guilt, shame and mental illness with young people – young people like me at that moment and young people like you.

As you've no doubt worked out by now, this is a book about 'mental health' – two words that can mean so much to so many. For some, the term is increasingly spoken about, acceptable, perhaps even fashionable. For others, they will be words that carry much judgement, pain, fear and shame. When we think of mental illness, we all have particular images that come to mind, but statistically one in four people has a mental illness and often these have no physical symptoms – but the fact that they are hard to spot doesn't mean

2

people aren't struggling, and mental health conditions can affect people of all ages, races and genders.

I wrote this book during the COVID-19 pandemic, which was a time of real uncertainty and isolation for many of us. A time when people's routines and structures were picked apart. And while the UK was certainly witnessing a mental health crisis before this, we saw the number of people struggling with their mental health skyrocketing during this time, and the aftermath of the pandemic has the potential to affect us for years to come. The figures show that 10 million people (8.5 million adults and 1.5 million children and young people) in England will need support for their mental health as a direct result of the pandemic over the next three to five years.[1] But because we know that so many mental health issues are kept secret, this is arguably just the tip of the iceberg of a much greater problem.

We must also remember that although one in four people may have a diagnosable mental illness, every single one of us has mental health. Throughout our lives we will work our way up and down a spectrum of mental health, experiencing periods when it is good and times when it is poor, the latter being no sign of weakness but just the reality – and that's before you throw in a global pandemic, modern societal pressures and more. And though we cannot attribute all poor mental health to the pandemic, we know that certain situations will have had a role to play in our mood and our health: eating disorders, for example, really thrived in the secrecy of being locked down as people found coping mechanisms or a way of dealing with the uncertainty without needing to talk about things.

Many of us will struggle with our own mental health to some degree or journey with someone else going through seasons of poor mental health, and it's likely that people will be picking this book up for different reasons. Some of you will simply have an interest in mental health; others will know someone who is struggling. Or maybe you have found yourself experiencing that dull ache in your stomach that so many of us sit with time and time again, for some reason unable to fully live the life we want. And, after all, didn't Jesus promise us that he has 'come that [we] may have life and have it to the full . . .'? So why do we still ache?

When it comes to faith and mental health, I know that I have found myself becoming frustrated with a lot of the narratives we hear that culminate in God's healing people in an instant. Though I *do* believe God can heal and we will all be healed eventually (more on that later), I falsely believed that the reason why God didn't just take my mental illness away was because of something I had done wrong. It's part of the reason I responded to altar calls as a young person by walking straight out of the meeting tent! I felt that I somehow needed to be better or more lovable or less complicated to be worthy of God's healing power. I thought that I was the only broken person around. My story isn't one of complete and instant healing (yet!) but of finding more freedom, love and hope on the journey.

So now a bit about me: my name is Hope Virgo (well, it's actually Jennifer Hope Virgo, but I go by my middle name, a slight frustration in itself as I often forget which name I have used at the bank, the doctor's or on my phone contract!). I am a full-time writer, speaker and mental health campaigner, leading a campaign called #DumpTheScales. The #DumpTheScales initiative is all about changing policy and practice concerning eating disorders. It is about making sure that funding is in place for treatment and that the right education is provided, and aims to ensure that people stop judging the severity of an eating disorder on the basis of a person's BMI (Body Mass Index). The campaign has seen me meeting MPs at the Houses of Parliament to talk, visiting Number 10 Downing Street and appearing on many national broadcasting outlets such as the BBC and Sky News to share my thoughts on eating disorders, exercise addiction and mental health more broadly. My campaigning is my passion and something that drives me every day to keep fighting the injustices that so many people face. And not just the injustices in service provision, but also the lack of people talking about what is actually going on for them. I think that so often people settle for where they are, with unhealthy behaviours, coasting through life not really that happy but just thinking that this is it and this is something that I am working to change. It's part of the reason I've written this book. The other part is that I think that, if we're not careful, our Christian faith – or how we wrongly understand it – has the power to hinder, to make us feel shame or embarrassment at times, as well as to help us, heal us and offer us hope.

I grew up going to church but gradually pulled away when I didn't have someone breathing down my neck, began rebelling and distanced myself even more. I have spent so much of my life in a cycle of self-doubt and self-hatred, sabotaging a lot of what happens, carrying guilt and shame from my past and never quite feeling good enough. It may be that you are in a similar situation right now or that you're feeling countless other emotions that you're pretty sure no one else will understand. I promise: you are not alone. I may not be fully healed yet but I am in an entirely different place from where I was, and my life has changed so much for the better since I was younger; each day I am getting better at managing my emotions, my mood and my own recovery. It's hard work, but I have every faith that you can get to this place too.

Throughout this book, we will be exploring some of the key themes in mental health and well-being and I will be speaking to a number of experts and church leaders about how our relationship with God can lead to the possibility of true freedom in the midst of our struggles. This book is not a replacement for therapy or medical assistance, but I hope it will aid you on your journey and help you to know that you are not alone.

It may be that you are currently feeling intense anger and frustration towards the Church, but I would encourage you not to project that anger onto God and, instead, to approach each fresh page with an open mind. As you read, do remember that these things take time and, while the apparently impossible is possible with God, allow yourself to work through this process at your own pace. It can also be good to go through the process with other people. I wonder, as you begin working your way through this book, whether you can find someone to chat to or even be accountable to if there are old patterns you are trying to break and new ones you are hoping to cultivate. It needs to be someone you trust, someone you can be vulnerable with and someone who can challenge you about things that aren't good and healthy for you. I couldn't recommend more highly having someone like this walking alongside you in your battle. When I returned to church (more on this to come too!), I identified a few people with whom I could be totally vulnerable. These people not only inspire me but motivate me to keep stepping forward into the light and in freedom. As we embark on this journey together, let's take a moment to think about who we can take with us.

I don't know what your story is, or what you or someone you love or care for is currently going through, but I pray that this book will open your eyes further to who God is. I pray that it will help you to plunge deeper into your faith and make a lifelong commitment to choose each day to move forward, trusting that God is good. We will be journeying together, in the hope that we can set one foot in front of another and become free from our past and feel empowered to make daily choices to walk boldly as conquerors into our future.

So let's start with a prayer:

Prayer

Dear God, thank you that you are the loving God; thank you that you are there for me and that you are working even when it feels as if you are not. I pray that, as I read this and work though the exercises, you can help me take steps to be totally free to live the life you have marked out for me. Amen.

1

Free from labels

'You are worthless! You couldn't possibly do that! You are fat! You are ugly!' The words echoed through my head as I sat there looking into the mirror. I was getting ready for a night out with my friends but my brain wouldn't settle down. This inner dialogue was getting louder and louder, plastering labels all over me. I knew where the labelling was going to end, and, sure enough, moments later: 'There is something wrong with you.' As it hit that landing point, I knew the only way to stop it there and then would be to drink my way through the evening, even though I was only just 15. I had always been the 'chatty', 'outgoing' friend, and even though my brain was at war in my head, I had to push on. I couldn't let anyone see what was really happening inside.

Whether they are words we like (such as 'chatty' and 'outgoing') or ones we loathe ('ugly', 'not enough'), labels are imprinted on us from the moment we are born by both ourselves and others. And, if we're not careful, these labels can form so much of who we are, how we think about ourselves and what we do that they go right to the heart of our identity, spilling out into our everyday actions, behaviours, responses and thoughts. For many of us, these labels may have come from our childhood or our family, but in a time when we share so much of ourselves on social media, we can feel the weight of so many labels as we become obsessed with showcasing our best selves and fall victim to the modern societal pressures that tell us that we are constantly not enough unless we look a certain way. Believe it or not, the seventh most Googled question in 2020 (and remember this was when the world witnessed the exposure of further racism and inequality in the wake of the pandemic and the death of George Floyd) was 'How to lose weight?' And the tenth most Googled 'Who?' question was 'Who has unfollowed me on Instagram?'[2]

For so many people who often feel stuck in feelings of failure and not being good enough, it can at times seem impossible to navigate life without self-destructing or without looking for an immediate quick fix. I know that, in my case, the labels I pinned on myself from an early age had a massive impact on how I saw myself and subsequently on the deterioration of my mental health. As I explain a bit more about where my struggles with my mental health began, I wonder whether you can take a moment to think about who you are, about what labels you may be 'wearing' – whether good or bad – and who you feel may have imprinted these on you. How is modern society making you feel about who you are? And why are you basing so much of your self-worth on your image?

Where it all began

I was born on 8 May 1990 as the third child in a Christian family. My sister Kate is three years old than me; my brother James two years older than me, my brother Samuel a year younger than me and my sister Mollie wasn't born until I was seven, safely slotting me into the 'middle child' position. We often joked about my having 'middle child syndrome', which is the belief that the middle children are often excluded or ignored. And while some of the associated traits are good – the ability to keep the peace, creativity, independence – if you look at the research on middle child syndrome, you will often read that the middle child is overshadowed and has rivalry with other siblings.[3] Whether or not it was intentional, I began to believe all these labels and, in many ways, allowed them to shape my identity, often acting up; I was always 'the naughty one'. It was these labels that fuelled so much of the narrative that I was to go on and tell myself as I got older.

Each Sunday morning, my mum would stand at the bottom of the stairs calling my siblings and me to hurry up and get in the car to go to church. I enjoyed the church community and had some lovely friends there, so it didn't bother me that it dominated my Sundays, but I very quickly learned that I had to act in a certain way to feel accepted there. Most weekends at church I was told off in front of everyone: 'Hope, just listen'; 'Hope, stop being bossy'; 'Hope, you shouldn't always be the group leader . . .' In the beginning I found it humiliating, shrinking back into my thick fleece wishing the world would swallow me up completely. After a couple of years of feeling 'too much' and as if I was always the odd one out, I started faking confidence, striding boldly into the church building in my baggy jeans or bright pink cords (I promise they were fashionable back in the day!), but the truth was I was painfully insecure. Before long, I would be setting my alarm early on a Sunday morning to give myself time to try on everything in my wardrobe, putting more and more emphasis on my appearance in an attempt to make myself feel good enough, before, more often than not, settling for a pair of tracksuit bottoms and a hoodie to hide the entirety of me.

I have heard wonderful stories of people finding a safe space in a church community (and in many ways I too have experienced this later in life), but for me at the time it felt like a place where I was labelled 'too much' and it didn't take long for school to become a place where I felt 'too little'. You see, my older sister, Kate, was undeniably brilliant and though I really looked up to her, it didn't take long for people to compare me unfavourably with her. I wasn't as smart as she was, or as hard-working. In an attempt to stop 'living in the shadow' of my older sister, my parents agreed that I should move to a different senior school from her. Here I had space to be me, and I loved joining every sports team going. At home I joked that I was the stupid one but at least I was good at sport, as if these two identities couldn't go hand in hand. But although I felt strong on the pitch, off it I still struggled to fit in with everyone else, never quite feeling 'cool' enough. One Saturday, I was so set on being like all the other girls that I became fixated on a certain black coat. I persuaded my mum to drive me all the way to the shops, rushed in, bought it and couldn't wait to wear it to school the following week – only for someone to make a comment about how I looked 'big' in it. I was heartbroken and never wore the coat again (in fact, I didn't wear a coat until I was 28 years old). I didn't know it at the time, but I was collecting all the labels that people stuck on me, whether at church or in school, until I felt that I wasn't lovable enough in either environment. I absorbed one central message (which, spoiler alert, is a *lie*): that there was something categorically wrong with who I was and so I needed to change myself to be loved.

Finding a friend

I didn't know what to do to fit in, to be accepted at church or in school, so I started to look elsewhere. And I found a friend who I thought at the time could help me: their name is anorexia. It may sound strange to call an eating disorder, a mental health condition, a 'friend', but like any good friend, in the middle of so much confusion about my identity and who I 'should' be, anorexia made me feel OK, acceptable, *loved*.

My disordered relationship with food began slowly, with restricting my calorie intake a bit, missing meals, trying new diets. But the more I did it, the better I felt, at least in the short term. It was like this best friend that helped numb my emotions and gave me a sense of control. And I loved it. I loved the value and purpose it gave me, helping me to just feel 'enough'. I longed for more of those feelings of validation, more of that control. I spent so much of my teen years trying to put on a front that no one really knew what was going on and, although I resented the energy it took to deal with it all, I just didn't know how else to manage my negative feelings, especially as I wouldn't talk to anyone about them. So instead of trying to find a way to open up, I focused on keeping up appearances. In a world where I was simply trying to fit in, my eating disorder served that purpose in making this feel more possible. If I felt pain or sadness, I skipped a meal and my new 'friend' pulled me close, distracting me by making me think about food and exercise until I felt that I had a handle on my destiny and identity.

The truth is, I had taken on so many labels, from 'too big to 'not good enough', that I felt I needed a plaster to make me feel better. The reality is we need more than just a plaster over these labels; we need to take off the old labels and put on the new God-given labels we were designed for. 'Mental health sufferer' can be another label we wear; we can feel like 'the sad one' or the 'broken one' or the 'not yet healed one', but the truth is there is so much that God says about our identity in the here and now that is the truest thing of all about us.

Of course, knowing this in theory is completely different from accepting it in practice. And so I wanted to sit down with Anna Hodges, host of a self-worth podcast, a woman who has been on a journey when it comes to finding her identity in God to explore how she has overcome her struggles with labels and identity in the face of adversity (which, I should flag here, includes sexual abuse. For those who will find such content triggering, please do skip 'Anna's story' or read it with a trusted friend). As we settled into our interview, Anna even joked that even a few years ago she would not have shown up for our meeting with greasy hair and no make-up on. Naturally, I was keen to hear the story of how she had become the confident and self-assured woman I saw before me.

Anna's story

Anna grew up in church and loved it. She and her friends were so wrapped up in church life that they practised preaching in front of their mirrors and sang worship songs into their hairbrushes. In her teens, Anna began modelling. At first she enjoyed the thrill of it, the affirmations from the man behind the camera telling her she was beautiful, that she was doing it right. But not long after starting she began comparing herself with everyone in the room; she never felt good enough. Such feelings were validated a few months later when a modelling manager told her: 'You will never be a professional model; you're not tall enough.'

Over the next few years, Anna took this subtle label, this non-factual opinion, of 'not enough' into her romantic relationships, three of which were hugely significant to her identity. The first was with a man she met when she was 20; they got engaged quickly but Anna had doubts about him. She decided to share these worries and concerns with someone at the church she was attending, but they dismissed them and told Anna she should still marry the person! Ten days before the wedding, Anna called the whole thing off and was then ignored by people in her church, leaving her feeling broken and alone. A few years later, Anna met Nick.[4] As in her previous relationship, Anna never felt 'enough' for him. Nick had an addiction to porn and as Anna didn't want him to be looking at other women, she allowed him to 'use' her to satisfy that need. During this time Anna was losing more and more confidence in who she was, and ended up getting a breast enlargement as one 'final attempt' to make herself feel good enough. When Nick and Anna were spending some time apart, she dated one more person, a young man she was working with on a film promo. One day, this man came over to work on the film and subsequently raped Anna. Heartbreakingly, Anna's self-esteem was so low at this point that she blamed herself completely. She ended up getting back together with Nick and they got married quickly, but having not worked through their problems. Nick's porn addiction got worse and they ended up getting divorced. The shame Anna felt in the wake of all this was huge. She had been labelled as 'divorced', 'victim' and 'not good enough' and constantly felt that people were judging her.

Anna felt trapped in a cycle of shame and guilt and was too afraid to talk to anyone about this. Even so, she didn't pull away from church life completely and ended up going to a Christian festival called Big Church Day Out. It was around this time that people kept having prophetic words for Anna, telling her to go to Bethel. Anna had grown up knowing about prophetic words, so while something inside her was hanging on to the hopeful things people were praying over her, she couldn't shake the judgement and the shame she was feeling; she didn't think she deserved such an opportunity. She sat on a hay bale in a tent, tears streaming down her face, listening to the song playing over the speakers, which repeated the lyrics: 'I need you, I want you.' In that moment, Anna felt closer than ever to Jesus as she sensed him singing those words over her and holding her in the middle of her hurt.

Anna ended up following people's prompting to go to Bethel School of Supernatural Ministry in California and, as she spent time studying and experiencing God and his love, she began to feel safe and secure. It was in this period that her identity really began to change, and she began to see how unique, significant and loved she really was. Though she had spent so much of her teens searching for beauty in herself and how she looked, she began to discover that she is beautiful because God made her, and that he made her more than enough as she is.

As I listened to Anna, she recalled a significant moment in finding her freedom from guilt and shame. 'I was at the Bethel School and attended this seminar on loving yourself well,' Anna shared with me. 'Honestly, I had even questioned whether to go, as I thought the whole thing seemed quite lame. One of the activities they got us to do was to stand naked in front of the mirror – we did this in private, not in front of everyone!' Anna went on: 'We were told to look at our bodies and be thankful. I had to quite literally stand there and work my way around my body, saying sorry for not loving a certain part, and then thanking that part for what it did. "Sorry, thighs, that I was unkind to you! Thank you, thighs, for carrying me."'

Putting on the mind of Christ

Hearing Anna share so eloquently and honestly her story of God's pursuing her and shaping her made me think: what happens if we don't have an experience like Anna's, where God is beckoning us in so clearly? What if we don't feel called to California or even that God is speaking clearly to us (I honestly did feel slightly jealous of that first part!)? But the truth is, the primary way God talks to us is through the Bible, in which he has many things to say about the labels and lies we tell ourselves and the words and promises he is speaking over us instead.

I don't know about you, but I constantly breathe lies over my body: my nose is too big, my legs too wide, my stomach a bit too round . . . I could go on. You may or may not have an eating disorder but we all have body image, and body image has such a huge impact on mental health. In fact, a study done by the Mental Health Foundation in 2019[5] showed that 37 per cent of teenagers felt upset, and 31 per cent felt ashamed, in relation to their body image. One in eight adults even experienced suicidal thoughts or feelings because of concerns about their body image. In your case, the lies you speak over yourself may be about your ability to do things: I'm not smart enough, or good enough. Or perhaps the lies are about your mental health itself: I'm never going to get better; I'm going to feel this way for ever. Whatever they are, you're not alone in struggling to tear off the negative labels we pin on ourselves, but in the Bible God invites us to move beyond letting these things dictate our identity and self-worth.

I was fortunate enough to sit down with Zeke Rink, who is a youth pastor in South West London and the Youth Network Associate Pastor for the national youth ministry Dreaming the Impossible. He had so much wisdom and knowledge to share on this topic. 'The reality is, you can change the way you look but no one can stop the body from changing. We get old, we age, our bodies change, but something shifts deep down when we become Christians,' Zeke explained. 'What is inspiring about the Bible is that it says so much about us! All you have to do is read through Scripture, for example John 1.12, which says we are children of God, or John 15.15, which says we are no longer servants but friends; Romans 5.1, which says we're justified through faith or 1 Corinthians 6.17, which says that whoever is united with God is one with him in Spirit. We can think the Bible is so daunting, but it is full of redemption and reconciliation.'

'We all know that what we dwell on and what we think about become totally consuming,' Zeke went on. 'So, instead of clothing ourselves in hatred for our bodies and who we are, perhaps we need to follow what it says in Romans 13.14, and instead "put on the mind of Christ" as we get dressed each day. Each day consciously say: "I know I am going to be faced with thoughts like 'I don't like myself', so what can I put on to tackle that?" In this verse in Romans, the apostle Paul talks about how secure Christ was, always in total connection with the Father, thinking what God thinks and doing what he sees the Father do. I know the world (as in society, culture, etc.) tells us one thing and most of us think "I wish X, Y, Z about my body", but what would it mean to be pleased with the way we have been created? This creation bears the image of God. Instead of getting fixated on the things we hate about ourselves, or those things we struggle with, let's challenge those thoughts and labels with not being true. I don't have time to think other than what God thinks of me. Imagine if you and I, as soon as thoughts came in that aren't in line with what God says, recognized them as lies and flushed out those thoughts with truth, thanking God that he has made us unique. Saying things like: "There is no one with the same bone structure as me, no one with the same hair colour; this is amazing!" What would life look like if we trusted God with how he has made us? If we loved ourselves as God made us?'

I looked over the Scripture passages that Zeke had suggested and began to think about my own spiritual disciplines: do I spend my time focusing on what the Bible says about me? In Romans 13.14, Paul tells us that we need to *put on* the mind of Christ, and this is a conscious decision. How often do I put on the mind of Christ? If I'm honest, on my harder days I can let my mind quite literally sabotage all my thinking. I get up, perhaps see an email from someone, look in the mirror or have a memory, and before I know it I have a one-way ticket to self-hatred and noticing everything wrong with me. It is in these moments that all those labels that have been imprinted on me seem to gather more and more evidence. This isn't just a day-to-day thing but can also be something that affects us when it comes to friendship groups or events we are attending. We may feel that someone hasn't adapted a situation to make it inclusive of us and, before we know it, we are on that one-way trip to finding more evidence for believing once again that it is something wrong with us. The truth is that if we are putting on underwear daily, surely we should be putting on the mind of Christ in that same conscious manner. The more we look to Jesus, the more we get rid of unhelpful thinking and the more we can step into our destiny with God. But, like any habit, it can take time, commitment, determination and practice until our thoughts and actions are so habitual that they happen subconsciously.

I used to really struggle with speaking the Bible's simple truths over me, from I am loved (John 3.16) to I am fearfully and wonderfully made (Psalm 139.14). If God really loved me, if I was created as a child of God, why was I struggling with a mental health disorder? Even so, as much as we can grapple with these questions (and I do continue to grapple and believe it is important to ask these things), this doesn't make the Bible any less true. I decided to start speaking these truths over myself. I remember when I first began: I was standing in the shower one morning and looked down at my body, and the first thing that came to mind was how disgusting I looked. But instead of pondering on that thought and allowing my mind to go into overdrive about it, I actively decided to take those thoughts captive and instead say these words over myself: 'I am enough; I am a masterpiece; God has a plan . . .' And the next day I did the same, and the next day, and so on. I began to declare truths and promises over myself!

Of course, it is important to know that although we actively have to take lies and labels captive in order not to let them begin to warp our God-given identity, we do not have to do this alone. We can invite the Holy Spirit to help us in all our efforts. As we read in Matthew 16.24 (MSG): 'You're not in the driver's seat; *I* am. Don't run from suffering; embrace it. Follow me and I'll show you how. Self-help is no help at all. Self-sacrifice is the way, my way, to finding yourself, your true self.'

Later in the book, we are going to look more closely at control and what it means to surrender our lives to God, but before we move on from here I want to suggest a few steps that might help you begin to take lies and labels captive and build your identity on God.

Practical steps

Step 1: Realize that the world is constantly changing

What it takes to 'fit in' will always change, whether that be body shapes that are deemed acceptable or clothes that are in fashion or behaviours that are considered 'cool'. We are all built to be unique, and embracing and celebrating our God-given attributes, gifts and fancies will give us steadfast confidence in an ever-changing world.

Step 2: Notice who is speaking into your life

Environments shape who we are, and it is important to recognize the ones that are good for us and the ones that aren't. For example, when it comes to my own disordered eating, I have friends who have an intense focus on dieting, casually bringing up how little they are eating or what they are doing to shrink themselves, and though I do not think God wants us to 'cut' these people out, it may be helpful to place boundaries around these relationships so we don't make ourselves vulnerable to negative thought cycles.

Step 3: Interrupt the thought

When you label yourself as something or think negative things about yourself, ask yourself: did God really say that? So many of the labels we have given ourselves are things that God never said. They are simply someone else's opinion of us. It might be easier to make a list of these things to help equip you when you are feeling tired too!

Step 4: Speak biblical truth over yourself

You may want to stand in front of the mirror and thank God for your body, as Anna did, or highlight key scriptures, like Zeke, and write them on sticky notes or save the words in your phone notes to look at through the day.

Prayer

Thank you that in you I am enough, that you make me who I am. I pray that you can help me to see who I am in you and that each day when my brain is difficult and makes me question myself and my identity, or when I sink back into the unhelpful labels that others have put on me, you can draw me closer and closer. I declare the truths of Scripture over myself and pray that you can help me keep my eyes focused on you. Amen.

2

Free from shame

I walked up to the front door and knocked; a woman opened it. She had long brown hair and wore a multi-coloured dress, and soon steered me into a room. I was just nine years old and, after a season of struggling to engage my emotions in a healthy way (as they often came out in tiredness or the 'naughty' behaviour I've already told you about), my parents had decided that I should speak to a therapist. Walking into the room, I saw two big chairs, a desk facing the garden, plants everywhere, books on the shelves; it looked a bit like a second-hand shop. I would soon find myself here every Thursday lunchtime to talk and complete activities.

I remember sitting there doodling on a piece of paper one day when she was talking to me. Soon she was telling me off for not being engaged and, to make things worse, at the end of my appointment she asked my mum to come in for a quick 'chat' so that she could share with her what had happened in our session. My face flushed and I could feel myself heating up. I melted into my body, trying to disappear. I had done something wrong, and I *felt* wrong. And, instead of processing this with the therapist, I felt angry and ashamed. Soon, my nine-year-old self decided the best thing to do was just to make things up, to tell the woman what I thought she wanted to hear.

Though I couldn't describe what I was feeling at the time, I know now that it was shame. 'Shame' is one of those words that I hated for so long and I never really knew why. It made me feel uncomfortable and disgusted. Whenever anyone mentioned it, I would get this sick feeling in my stomach, a dull ache that told me something wasn't quite right. I wonder what thoughts and feelings it sparks for you. The definition of 'shame' in the dictionary is 'a painful feeling of humiliation or distress caused by the consciousness of wrong or foolish behaviour'. Brené Brown, an American professor, lecturer, author and podcast host, describes shame as an 'intensely painful feeling or experience of believing that we are flawed and therefore unworthy of love and belonging' that affects the way we interact with the world. Preacher and speaker Christine Caine explains in her book *Unashamed* that where 'guilt' makes us feel we *did* something wrong, 'shame' makes us feel 'I *am* something wrong', making us feel 'small, unwanted and unloved'.[6] Shame is something that I carried for so much of my life, trapping me inside my thinking, until I eventually found a way out of it.

Something wrong

Though I started struggling with my mental health and disordered relationship with food at an early age, there was another incident that happened to me in my early teens that took my feeling of shame to a whole new level. Like Anna's story, which I shared with you earlier, this part of my journey features sexual abuse, so if this is too hard for you to read now, do please skip this section or read through it with a trusted friend.

It all began quite quickly. I first saw him on a Sunday morning, talking to some of the other boys at Youth Club. I could never quite work out why he came along to the group: he wasn't quite old enough to be a proper leader, but he wasn't young enough to be a member. Over the next few weeks, I began talking to him. For some reason, everyone seemed to look up to him. He had an air of control and authority surrounding him. Over the next few weeks, our communication seemed to build – texts, then emails, each time getting longer and longer. At first, I liked the attention. I saw myself as this short, frumpy girl speaking to an older boy and it was exciting – the sort of thing that happens in a movie. Then things became uneasy.

As our communications got longer and later, I became more and more unsure, but by this point I felt stuck. I hated much of what he was writing to me but for some reason I kept going back to him, kept replying, kept sharing so much of myself with him: things I hadn't felt able to share with anyone before. As I did, he began to become more controlling, telling me negative things about my family, that I should be acting in a certain way and that it didn't matter that my mum didn't like him because we were 'meant to be together'. Throughout it all, I blamed myself for getting into this position and I didn't know how to get out.

I won't ever forget the first time 'it' happened. We were driving back from church, and he pulled over to the side of the road, hidden from passers-by, and asked me to kiss him, before slowly putting my hand on his crotch. He told me to touch it and then said it would feel nice if I put my mouth on it. I didn't know what to do. Before long, he was pushing my head down over it; I hated it and I felt sick, but I was too afraid to say anything. As he drove off again my eyes filled with tears, and, as I got out of the car, he said: 'Don't tell anyone about what happened; you don't want to get into trouble.' Throughout the evening, he sent more messages telling me that my parents didn't really love me and that they would never understand our relationship. What I didn't understand at the time was that this was all part of the grooming process so that I would do everything he wanted. And, for a time, I did. Sometimes afterwards he would cry, making me feel to blame, as if it was all my fault. I never cried; what was the point? But inside I was hurting so much, physically and emotionally. Other times, I was so fearful as we drove off after church to our 'secret spot' that I would clam up as he reached to the other side of the car. I'd distract myself by planning my meals for the week in my head, seeking to control the things I could while everything was spinning.

The shame was so great that it seeped into every part of me. I remember standing in church one evening, trying to sing my praises to God but finding nothing but cries coming out. Soon a friend came to join me and, just as I was about to open up to her, he arrived; it was as if he had a radar for when I was about to let someone else in on 'our secret'. He told my friend that she could go and he would sit with me instead, reminding me not to tell anyone the truth. There in that church, my relationship with God began to break down. I didn't feel able to be in the same space as God, asking for things, when my life seemed so messy. I didn't know how I could sit there and be still, worship and pray when I was carrying this disgusting secret around. Luckily, over the summer he got bored with me, letting me go. But it would take many more years for me to let go of the guilt and shame.

The shame game

Shame can come in all shapes and sizes, affecting our lives in a multitude of ways. You don't have to go through a form of abuse to feel shame; many things might have caused you to have this feeling. Whatever has led to the shame, it has the power to leave the same mark, and the scary thing about shame is that it has the potential to shape a person's entire life, especially if we seek to ignore it and instead resort to unhealthy coping mechanisms. I don't know your specific story or the story of your loved one, but it doesn't matter what society tells us we should or shouldn't be ashamed of: if you feel shame, it's vital that something is done about it.

Before we delve deeper into this topic, I would love to encourage you to reflect a bit on where you are on your own journey. I realized that, even ten years after I was discharged from a mental health hospital (more on this later), I still had a lot of work to do when it came to the role of shame in my life. Not only was the shame causing me to shrink in so many areas, but it also left me hating my body. When I realized this, I wanted an instant fix, to banish shame from my mind and life completely, buying every self-help book out there, but it takes time. And trust me when I say I know how frustrating that is. As we've already seen, the Bible tells us that self-help alone isn't the answer, but I didn't feel that God was answering either. Why was my recovery so slow? Why didn't he just fix me? Surely he is powerful enough? I wanted to sit down with someone who had journeyed closely with Jesus for years to pose some of these questions to her and see whether she had any more advice to offer people like me who want to be rid of shame for good.

I first met Jemima Haley about two years ago in an unassuming Caffè Nero near Clapham Junction. As I approached the café, I had no idea what to expect and was deliberating whether to just turn back and go home. I was 29 years old and hadn't been to church properly since I was around 17. I wouldn't have called myself a Christian at this point but I still wanted some answers when it came to faith. I had emailed someone at a large church called Holy Trinity Brompton (HTB) whom I had met around a decade ago and said that I would appreciate having someone to talk to, mainly because I naively felt that if I met someone who really believed in God and got them to pray for me, my problems would all then disappear. I walked into the café, sat down and flicked out my phone, just trying to settle myself, but in the July heat I soon began to sweat. Then a lovely woman approached me and introduced herself. She had a calmness about her, and it was one that had me splurging my entire life story to her for the next 35 minutes. It was only a few months later, back at HTB, when I heard Jemima's story, and it was packed full of so much wisdom when it came to finding freedom from guilt and shame that I knew I wanted to interview her for this book.

'I was born in the United Kingdom but raised in Ghana and remained there until I was about eight years old,' Jemima explained to me. 'The reason I had moved over there was that my mum was struggling as a single parent. During my time in Ghana, I moved around between different families. When I was eight, I came back to the UK and moved in with my mum and my half-brother (whom I had not met until this point). I gradually began to feel settled and as if I was part of this family, and over the next few years I worked out what it was like to live in London. When I went to university, my mum got really ill. During this time I was her primary carer, and though my friends told me that I shouldn't be taking on that role, I knew that if I didn't and something happened to her, I would feel really guilty. After my mum passed away, I began going to counselling. At the beginning, I was really embarrassed about going, but it became a vital tool for me in moving forward.'

As I listened to Jemima talk about initially being embarrassed about seeking help, I realized that this is so often the case when it comes to shame and our own mental health; if we're not careful, this shame will trap you in a cycle of not being able to ask for help because you think somehow it's your fault or you should be strong enough to deal with it. Then there comes the shame over being so angry with God for not preventing what is hurting you. As Jemima went on, she explained: 'Moving away from things that have hurt us comes from accepting that hurt and pain, saying this has happened and allowing it to boost our future.'

Jemima then shared that although she prayed about her counselling and believes that God has the power to heal us, it didn't and *doesn't* always change the reality of what she might be currently going through. 'Sometimes the most benefit I received from praying was gaining an inner sense of peace about the reality. It always calmed my heart even if it did not change the circumstances I was in. Sometimes we treat prayer as a genie in a bottle, and then we doubt God when we don't get everything on our wish list. But prayer is so much more than that; it is about bringing us closer to God, developing that relationship with him.'

For me, so much of my anger and frustration with God has been wrapped up in prayers not being answered the way I wanted them to be, but here was Jemima exhibiting something of which I think I really needed to remind myself: that even if things didn't change externally, it wasn't because she didn't have enough faith. It wasn't because God didn't love her enough. And he was still faithful about meeting her in the middle of the pain and the middle of the process. And though God *can* heal us in an instant, quite often he invites us to walk slowly and closely with him through the pain. I don't know about you, but doing anything slowly can feel so foreign to what we are used to in our instantaneous culture. Society tells us that we can get 'overnight success' or that we can move from A to B with ease. But the reality for many of us is that the really good things in life, such as cultivating deep relationships, take time and a bit of effort on our part too. Tim Stilwell, the vicar of St Dionis Church at Parsons Green, speaks about this brilliantly, explaining that if we were doing a marathon, we wouldn't expect to go from nought to running 26 miles in a day, and recovery from any mental health issue is no different. In recovery from mental illness, or periods of struggling with poor mental health or thought cycles of shame, we need to build in a few changes and progress from that space and then build in a few more healthy changes, and so on. It can be draining, exhausting and hard work at times, but the more we 'train', the easier it will get.

When it comes to shame and our mental health, having people around us who will speak the truth and point out shame's impact on our life is so important. I am fortunate enough to have had a friend do this for me, and its impact was life-changing. My friend spoke out plainly about some of my behavioural responses to situations. Because of the shame that I have carried, I have moments when I self-destruct, push people away; when the feeling that something is really wrong with me gets all-consuming. I take this out on the people closest to me, people who shouldn't be blamed for my past. Sometimes my friends experience the effects of my shame and insecurities and when they do, even if it feels uncomfortable for both of us, it is always helpful to hear about it (in the long term!). The reality is that, even if it is hard to hear (although people say it in a loving way), what I realized time and time again was that if a person didn't say something, I would probably mull over my self-pity and shame for goodness knows how long, allowing the impact of my past, and the shame that I have felt, to become something that can affect my behaviour and my mental well-being every day.

Freedom from shame

The important thing to remember when we are experiencing feelings of shame is that shame was never part of God's plan; God never wanted us to have to live with it. We can read the creation account in the book of Genesis in the Bible and learn how God created human beings, Adam and Eve in the Garden of Eden, in his image: a complete masterpiece. In Genesis 2.25 (NIV), it says: 'Adam and his wife were both naked, and they felt no shame.' I personally think the fact the notion of being 'unashamed' is mentioned so early on not only shows that our loving God intended us to be shame-free, but also demonstrates the absolute power of this emotion and the potential stranglehold shame can have on us.

The problem was – and I'm sure many of you have heard this story before – that the devil then came to tempt Adam and Eve, as we read:

> Now the serpent was more crafty than any of the wild animals the Lord God had made. He said to the woman, 'Did God really say, "You must not eat from any tree in the garden"?' The woman said to the serpent, 'We may eat fruit from the trees in the garden, but God did say, "You must not eat fruit from the tree that is in the middle of the garden, and you must not touch it, or you will die."'

Giving in to temptation, Eve ate some of the fruit from the one forbidden tree and gave some to Adam, and it was at this moment that the Scriptures say: 'Then the eyes of both of them were opened, and they realized they were naked; so they sewed fig leaves together and made coverings for themselves.' At this point sin entered the world, and it is this sin that keeps us from God. That sin and shame that so often keep us trapped. But the good news is that God didn't leave us there. Moving beyond Genesis, we start to see passages throughout the Bible emphasizing the power that Jesus has to break shame: 'He was despised and rejected by men, a man of suffering who knew what sickness was. He was like someone people turned away from; He was despised, and we didn't value Him' (Isaiah 53.3, HCSB). Crucifixion was the lowest of the low and Jesus went through that for us so that we could find freedom from shame. In Hebrews 12 (NIV) we read:

> Therefore, since we are surrounded by such a great cloud of witnesses, let us throw off everything that hinders and the sin that so easily entangles. And let us run with perseverance the race marked out for us, fixing our eyes on Jesus, the pioneer and perfecter of faith. For the joy set before him he endured

the cross, despising the shame, and sat down at the right hand of the throne of God.

Sometimes we make the shame that we feel – our sins, our feelings, our struggles – so much bigger than Jesus and what he did for us (I know I do this), but the Bible speaks the truth that we can be free because of him.

In Ephesians 5 we read about the power of bringing sin and shame into the light, confessing our sin to Jesus and the people with whom we are in community. If we name those behaviours, it helps stop their power taking over. Thinking about my own unhealthy coping mechanisms, I can see that these were attempts to hide my shame, but as soon as I began to bring them out into the open, I was able to step forward, out of the darkness of my own thoughts. I was able to start to express the shame in a healthy way.

We need to get to a place where we are allowing ourselves to be vulnerable with God, to cry out to him. In the Psalms, David does just this: he cries out; he shares his fears and his sadness. And do you know what? Even if our situation doesn't instantly change, even if we don't immediately hear from God, we know that God hears us. In this moment, when you are travelling through your wilderness, whatever that might look like for you, hold on to all those times in the past when God has been faithful, when he has delivered on a promise. I find making lists really helpful at these moments, especially when I am lying awake at night potentially ruminating over the current situation.

In my case, the shame made me feel small, as if there was something wrong with me, as if I was unlovable, and that everyone was going to leave me – ironically causing me to push people away before they could hurt me. In hindsight, I don't think I was *ready* to get rid of the shame in the early stages of my recovery. It had become such a massive part of my identity, and while I believed it could shift for others, I wasn't sure it would for me. In fact, I was convinced that maybe my shame was too entrenched to be shifted at all; I had lived with it for most of my life, and it didn't always affect me as long as I didn't think about it. I had my own coping mechanisms and was convinced that if I told anyone, they might reject me. Deep down, I was terrified of opening a can of worms, of pouring my heart out and nothing being resolved. Even so, the Bible makes it very clear that because of the sacrifice of Jesus, there is no place for shame in our new lives with Christ.

In John 4 verses 1–26 we read one of my favourite stories (I encourage you to grab your Bible or Google the story now). In it, Jesus encounters a woman by a well. Jesus asked her for a drink; historically a Jewish man would not have spoken to a Samaritan woman because interaction between the two was frowned upon. The Samaritan woman had come alone to get water in the heat of the day; perhaps because of her past with its multiple marriages, she chose to visit the well when there would be less fear of judgement from others.

"The Samaritan woman said to him, "You are a Jew and I am a Samaritan woman. How can you ask me for a drink?" (verse 9, NIV). But Jesus pressed in further, explaining that if she knew who was asking for the water, she would not question it.

Jesus didn't turn away from her when he saw this woman who was so gripped by shame; he felt it with her. The story shows this real love and forgiveness from Jesus meeting us where we are. Jesus didn't come for the rich, for the people who seem to have it all together, but for every single one of us, no matter what our background. It is amazing when you stop and think that this story is in the Bible, and it is one of the longest encounters recorded there, which emphasizes on so many levels the importance of this conversation.

The story also shows us that the only way to real freedom, to real life, is through God. We see examples of this healing power throughout the Bible, especially in those places where we least expect it; those places where others have tried to hide their shame. In Luke 8 verses 43–5, there is the woman who had suffered a discharge of blood for over a decade. She was too ashamed to come forward when she heard about Jesus healing people, so instead touched his cloak. In these stories, we see not only shame at play, but pride stopping people from reaching out for support. Pride and shame cause us to hide inside certain behaviours, hide in our 'safe spaces', perhaps hiding away from God until we are 'fixed'. In order to break the power of shame, we need to make our way to Jesus. Like so many others before us. If we go to Jesus then we are promised life to the full. It is these promises that we can hold on to (2 Corinthians 1 verse 20).

This is all well and good in theory, some of you might be thinking, but how do I really break the power of shame in my life in practice? What would it even *look* like? I had the pleasure of sitting down with the wonderful Rachel Hughes, Pastor of Gas Street Church in Birmingham, and posing some of these questions to her.

'When we are in shame, whatever has been triggered, the desire to self-protect arises,' Rachel shared with me openly. 'We fall into addiction. We want to control or numb. But the paradox is that when we numb the shame, we are also numbing the good stuff. As individuals, we have to choose to put our real and authentic self on the table. I have noticed that when I choose to be vulnerable, it unlocks shame. The lie of shame is: "It's just me; I am the only one and if they really knew, they wouldn't like me."'

'There is a woman in our church, and she was living in shame,' Rachel went on. 'She felt she didn't fit in as she was so consumed by shame, but within a couple of weeks she heard someone talking openly and sharing vulnerably. After this, the woman felt able to share some of what was going on with her. She then began the journey of breaking away from the shame. It is the learned practice of knowing that what is on the other side is really good. I have learned that when I surrender to God, it brings me more life and freedom. It feels counterintuitive, as releasing fear may seem to be bringing yet more fear. Trust that the view from jumping out of a plane is going to be good. When I am in a space of shame, control can feel comfortable and safe, but instead it is a prison. The prison can seem so safe that stepping out of it can feel hard and scary and daunting. But I know that when I have let go of the fear of opening up, what's on the other side is so much better. There is so much more freedom and life. And people start to recognize this. Our most beautiful self internally and externally is our most surrendered self.'

As I listened to Rachel speaking, I could relate to so much of what she was saying. I was absolutely terrified of surrendering my shame to God; so afraid that I preferred resorting to my daily coping mechanisms, my very own 'prison', when stepping outside them would lead to so much more freedom. I thought I had a handle on my shame, but in reality it was making me doubt myself, feel unworthy and unlovable and, at times, act like it too. You might have your own coping mechanisms, and while you know deep down that you aren't happy, you believe you can sort it out through your behaviours. You push people away so that they don't get close enough; you punish yourself with exercise, maybe resort to drinking, drugs, busyness, fixing others, doing everything you can to mask those feelings, and even though you know that it's having an impact on your mental well-being you keep doing it. You keep treading water in that position. It might be that, like me, part of you felt you didn't even deserve to surrender the shame.

I posed this question to Zeke Rink, Youth Network Associate Pastor at Dreaming the Impossible: 'What if we don't feel we deserve this to be changed?' Naturally, Zeke came up trumps with his answer, explaining that this is exactly the story of the Gospel: none of us deserved Jesus' dying on the cross, but he did it anyway because he cares about us that much. As Zeke explained: 'We need to keep going back to God with all these issues. We aren't meant to be beating ourselves up about our past but recognizing that stuff and challenges happen in our lives, and that as we give our lives over to Jesus we are saved and transformed by the Spirit of God. The reality is, this doesn't always happen overnight, but it is a process of healing, of forgiving ourselves, of opening ourselves up to Jesus.'

So, practically, what can we do to move on from our shame? From our past? To help ourselves know that we are enough?

Practical steps

Step 1: Recognize and rewrite

We can rewrite the script in our head, recognizing those things that we have told ourselves are fact (even when they aren't) and speaking truths such as 'I am good enough' over ourselves. When shame makes us feel that something is wrong with us, it's important to interrupt the shameful thought and look at the evidence! If you find this hard to do, write down everything you feel about yourself and then find a scripture that counteracts each negative thought.

Step 2: Be honest with God

I have a journal constantly on the go and sometimes when I don't know how to speak things out, I write them down, sometimes even scribbling on the page. We can be honest with God, offering him our sadness, anger, joy and lament, and we are given a scriptural blueprint for this in the Psalms. You could write your own psalm to God, calling out to him about your situation and what you (honestly) want him to do about it.

Step 3: Counselling

As Jemima advocates in this chapter, counselling can be very helpful. Back in 2019, I chose to go back to therapy, and having the space to process things was vital. Through talking to someone, I was able to move from a position where I blamed myself for the abuse detailed in this chapter and realize that it was not my fault. Talking to a friend or family member might be just what you need in your circumstances, but sometimes a professional offers particularly valuable insights.

Prayer

God, sometimes I am afraid of opening up, afraid of hurting myself and those around me more than I feel I already am. I am scared that nothing will change and that I will still be trapped in my shame. I don't know where to start. Please help, God; come near to me. I know you are the God who saves and died so that we could be free. Holy Spirit, come.

3

Free from fear

When you think of fear, what's the first thing that comes to mind? The spider scuttling across the floor, some sort of reptile, being in an enclosed space or finding yourself at a great height? If so, you're not alone. At least 60 per cent of adults have admitted to having some sort of 'unreasonable' fear.[7] I'll confess, I have a fear of heights to the extent where I went on a date on the London Eye and spent the entire time curled up in a ball on the bench in the middle of the pod! And above and beyond the 'traditional' phobias, there are so many other things that grip our society with fear. In our social-media-obsessed culture that too often tells us we should look, act and behave a certain way, it is no surprise that so many of us live with a fear of not being liked, not being skinny enough, happy enough, loved enough . . . simply *enough*.

Before we explore further how we can become 'free from fear', I want you to take a moment to think about what you are most afraid of. And I mean *really* afraid of. You don't need to tell anyone else, not unless you want to, so try to be honest with yourself. I'll go first: my biggest fear, which underlies all the labels and shame I have already spoken about, is the fear of abandonment, the fear that if I show my entire self to someone, I'll be abandoned, rejected, not loved.

Fear is such a huge emotion, which has the power to cripple us or to propel us forward; to motivate us or to stop us in our tracks. A healthy amount of fear can tell us to run from real danger or make sensible, well-informed decisions based on the circumstances in which we find ourselves. But if we let our fears run wild, we begin to create a false narrative that can control us, telling ourselves to retreat to our comfort zones and never step out in faith. We can start to allow worst-case scenarios to dictate our internal dialogue until the 'what ifs?' become our reality. Through my battles with the fear of rejection and the many ways I've sought to keep this fear in check, I've discovered that we have a choice: we can let fear dictate our decisions or we can challenge our fears, facing them with faith.

Trying to control the fear

I was 14 years old when I realized that helping others was my passion, and I jumped at the chance to volunteer at a Christian event called Soul in the City. This five-day outreach programme saw 20,000 young people take to the streets of London to paint, clean, talk to people and help the community. It was just months after I had cut all ties to my abuser, and as I stood painting the side of a local basketball court, another unhelpful narrative reared its ugly head: 'You know that fear of rejection you feel, Hope? If you continue to help people, continue to volunteer, then you will be accepted . . .'

This narrative followed me around all summer, morphing and attaching itself to other situations in my life. Although the physical abuse had stopped, it was as if the memory of what had happened – all the hurt, the pain and blaming myself – was playing tricks with my already fragile mind. Whereas it started with helping other people, it then became about other things. 'You know this fear of rejection you feel, Hope? If you can just get that boy to like you, then you'll be accepted . . .' And so I spent a lot of energy trying to do just that. I began a cycle of moving from one boy to another as a way of numbing the pain, but also to help me feel that I was taking ownership and control of my own sexuality. I would fix my eyes on a boy, perhaps even pursuing two at the same time, and once I had got them to like me, to affirm me, the fear of rejection subsided – at least in the short term. Sitting there kissing a boy I liked, I was able to tell myself that maybe what had happened to me wasn't because I was disgusting, that maybe people would accept me exactly how I was.

The problem was that in trying to be accepted by everyone, I was losing sight of who *I* was altogether; I was once again making myself what I thought others wanted me to be. Before long, I was becoming more and more like one of those Russian dolls: different versions of me, breaking apart whenever I needed them to – the well-behaved, outgoing churchgoer, the constantly rebelling drinker, the sports player, the one who messed about at school, causing havoc in lessons, and then me. The broken one, battling with food and an exercise addiction. The one who, despite those exterior guises, was often staring back at me from the mirror. But my fear of rejection meant I was too scared to show anybody *that* part of me.

I was feeling more and more out of control, but I still thought I had the perfect solution. Little did I know that my 'best friend', anorexia – the one that made me feel better each time I restricted my calorie intake or exercised for an extra half an hour – was becoming more like a lover than any of the boys I tried to pursue during this time. We were becoming obsessed with each other; I was fixated on numbers: calories in, calories burned, meals skipped. They say hindsight is 20/20, and as I look back at my diary entries from around this time, I can see now that the thing I was doing to try to control things was now controlling me:

> I weighed myself today with pyjamas and wet hair and had lost weight. Winner! I am going to weigh myself at 8 p.m. on the dot each night now.

I put on this happy face for others, but I am hurting so much. I need to just forget it for now. I am now going to become a vegetarian.

I am going to eat less tomorrow as I want to lose weight. If I lose weight, I will be happy and more liked and then I won't have to worry about people rejecting me.

Exposing fears

As we've already seen, mental illnesses come in many forms, and they are not all rooted in our fears. This said, fear can have an obvious impact on our mental well-being and sense of self and, for me personally, my controlling response to fear had no small part to play in developing my eating disorder. Control is a very natural response to fear, but we know that the Bible tells us: 'Perfect love drives out fear, because fear has to do with punishment. The one who fears is not made perfect in love' (1 John 4.18, NIV). So why do so many of us feel afraid? And how can we find that peace that we are promised in the Bible? How do we get rid of our need for control? I posed this very question to Jon Toms, a wellness coach, and he just smiled, promptly telling me: 'I still have mine . . .'

'Fear breeds a need for control,' Jon explained further. 'When we feel fear, we try to respond in a way that makes us feel safe. And while it might seem logical, we know that there is often a deep-rooted issue. And although none of this is a quick fix, the more love we let in, the better. Community is the key for me! We weren't created to "do life" alone, so not only do we need to find people around us that we can be vulnerable with, but we also need to find a safe place and intimacy with God. That place where we can really receive what God freely offers us. I call it "receive mode". Is my heart attentive? Am I positioned to receive? And on those days when I'm more at risk of getting overwhelmed with fear, I make sure I am checking in with God more. Interacting with him and listening to his truth about me.'

As I listened to Jon, I realized that I have too often let my fear drive out God, rather than allow God to drive out fear. Have you found yourself in a similar situation? When you may be having a 'good day' and feel open to God, in 'receive mode', and then a worry comes in and soon you are putting distance between yourself and God, grappling for control? I am sure I am not the only one who has gone for hours, days, sometimes even weeks without interacting with God when I am weighed down with worries. And, instead of finding comfort in the sense of control, I find my mood slips lower and I become even more afraid, in my case projecting the worries onto my body, consequently causing more fear of judgement. When I am in this situation, I do not see community as the answer but as a place rife with comparison. Nowhere do I feel this more than through social media, where we see people projecting the 'finished product' without sharing what they are going through 'behind the scenes'. As Jon Toms so correctly points out, community can instead be a place of safety, of vulnerability, where we can bring our fears into the light, seeing their power break in front of God and others.

Rachel Hughes also had a unique insight into how to reframe how we see fears, identifying some of her own need for control as an idol, something that we perhaps even subconsciously find taking the place of God himself. 'Idolatry sounds so old-school,' Rachel explained to me. 'But when you really break it down, our idols are rooted in our fears: what if I am not beautiful? What if I am not thin? This fear leads to "worshipping" the idol of beauty, or size, etc. By nature, I don't mind taking risks, but my fear is of not being enough. And, more often than not, about the way I look. The idols create this fragile sense of control and so when I feel afraid that I'm not enough, the temptation is to fall back on control mechanisms.' Thankfully, Rachel has found a discipline that really helps her let go of this need to seize control: 'The discipline of repentance is so important to me; in my counselling they take me through these prayers in each session that have been so powerful in giving me space to renounce idols in my life; for example, laying down the idol of beauty, of being skinny. It has been pretty life-changing.'

Before we dive into what the Bible says about fear and control, it is important to note that not all fears will lead back to idolatry – and certainly not when what we experience is above and beyond anxiety-induced periods of poor mental health and instead an identified mental illness. As Claire Williams, Associate Lecturer at Regents Theological College and a PhD candidate in Practical Theology at Durham University, explained to me when we sat down to discuss this topic: 'If someone is unwell, for example calorie counting or self-harming, then we need to be really careful about talking about sin! If they are feeling that the Spirit is convicting them, we can certainly pray for help. But this is not a blanket statement that this is sinful, because we don't know. It is important to be aware of idols in the sense of what we are putting first. As individuals, we can reflect on this and perhaps work out where something is sitting in our priorities. Once we have found that out, we can look at what we are perhaps missing instead: is it control, fear, issues of trust?'

As someone who has lived with an eating disorder for a long time, I found what Claire shared with me next really encouraging: 'We have got to go easier on ourselves; God isn't about picking apart every detail with us. Perhaps it is more about saying: "I have been ill, I am still hoping to be better, and I know that God doesn't condemn." It might be worth framing it in other ways to stop that thinking escalating. When that thinking does start to esca-late, we could instead focus on saying thank you to God for not condemning us! We could try to change our thinking and practices; so, instead of doing a certain behaviour, every time we are tempted to do it we pray, taking up those actions that are bringing us closer to God. Remember that God has saved us, and so we don't need to dwell on these behaviours but instead do something proactive to stop those thoughts.'

Learning to trust

The truth is, we will all face fears in this lifetime, and we know that God doesn't want us to get stuck in the cycle of trying to keep a lid on our fears ourselves. In 2 Timothy 1.7 (ESV) it says: 'For God gave us a spirit not of fear but of power and love and self-control.' Once again, this reminds us that we have a choice: choose fear or choose faith. But how do we do this in practice? How do we keep ourselves in 'receive mode'? How do we know when to recognize our fear and need for control as idols and repent and turn back to God? The answer, I think, lies in trust.

Trust God. Sounds pretty simple, right? Trusting people comes easily to some of us, but is much harder for others. As I spoke to a fellow mental health campaigner, Helen Missen (a carer representative for F.E.A.S.T., a global community of parents and those who support parents in families affected by eating disorders), she explained that: 'Trusting God was definitely easier as a child, but if I don't trust God, what is the point? I look around where I live and see the buds on the trees and it is amazing – how does this happen? How can we not believe? I trust in something I can't see but I also trust God because I have seen him work miracles and seen him stand alongside me. I have seen him guard my children and be by my side. At times it is harder to trust, and that is life, but I have to have faith and that is non-negotiable. I pray, and I hold on to the nature of God.' Helen has seen miracles and had moments in her life that she can hold on to as evidence that God is trustworthy. Thankfully for those of us who find it harder to see tiny miracles in everyday life, whether owing to our mental health or to something else, the Bible is full of passages that tell us about the trustworthy nature of God.

Firstly, in Psalm 33.4 (NIV) we see that we can trust the words of the Bible itself: 'For the word of the LORD is right and true; he is faithful in all he does.' In Psalm 18.30 (NIV), we read that we can trust God's behaviour: 'As for God, his way is perfect: The LORD's word is flawless; he shields all who take refuge in him.' We see that if we turn to him, if we are honest with him about our fears, he will never turn away from us: 'For the LORD is good and his love endures forever; his faithfulness continues through all generations' (Psalm 100.5, NIV). And that, no matter what we have been through or how dark things seem now, if we turn to him, God will honour his promise to us to work 'for the good of those who love him, who have been called according to his purpose' (Romans 8.28, NIV). I've picked out only four scriptures here, but the Bible is full of countless reasons and promises that God is trustworthy. Declaring them over ourselves can remind us to trust God fully with our fears and with whatever happens next. I know that I have been through times of trusting God with everything, to reclaiming so-called self-control over my circumstances. When I have a bad day, my brain will begin its ruminations, going over and over things late into the night. Even though it doesn't always feel like it, I do have a choice in those moments. I can choose to listen to my brain, to resort to those unhealthy controlling behaviours to manage the fear. Or I can embrace the pain, sit with the discomfort with God, and see what might be on the other side of it.

Telling God about our fears and learning to trust him is a powerful first step, I believe; the best one we can ever take. And yet, as well-being coach Jon Toms said earlier in this chapter: 'We weren't created to "do life" alone.' Another choice we have to make when facing fear is whether we're going to let anyone else into it. I've found that sharing my fears with trusted friends and family members is a game changer. For me, the starter has always been something like: 'I am struggling with this.' Once it is out in the open, although it doesn't become a magic silver bullet to fix things, it helps. The enemy has a field day when things are kept secret and this secrecy tends to make us feel even more guilty and shameful about that behaviour. We are reminded of this in Ephesians 5.11–14 (NASB), where it says '. . . all things become visible when they are exposed by the light, for everything that becomes visible is light.'

And remember, what is on the other side of fear is better than anything we *think* might be helping us in the moment: 'I don't want to live in a prison,' Pastor Rachel Hughes told me. 'My daughter has battled with anxiety – she is doing really well – but when it is at its worst, the fear will stop her taking risks and choosing experiences that bring her joy. I sometimes have to ask myself: "Am I going to let the fear rob me of this joyful experience?"'

Practical steps

Step 1: Recognize your fears and challenge your coping mechanisms

Sometimes life can go so fast, and we need to make decisions so quickly, that we don't even recognize that fear is driving us. For some, the fear of letting people down can lead to burnout; for others, their fears are a healthy part of recognizing sensible paths to take. Take a moment to stop and recognize the role of fear in your life – is it a healthy one? Are you trying to control it? If the latter, take some time to look at your thinking patterns or behaviour. Are there unhealthy coping mechanisms at play? Think about the last time you felt out of control, consumed by fear. What did you do in that moment? Where is your comfort? Where do you put your trust? Do you feel comfortable naming that or does it feel a bit yucky to say it out loud? Write it down and take a moment to start to bring these behaviours into the light. Remember, Jesus is right there alongside you.

Step 2: Identify idols and repent

This will not be appropriate for everyone: remember, mental illness is not a sin. For some of us, however, our fears and need to control may expose an idol in our life: something we are intentionally or unintentionally letting take the primary position of God. If this rings true to you, why not think about what Rachel Hughes said about this: identify these idols, bring them to God and say sorry for them. Remember that in Jesus you are already forgiven. He died for our sins.

Step 3: Immerse yourself in Scripture

I heard a podcast recently by Hillsong UK pastor Julie Galanti, encouraging us to make a list of all our worries, working out what we can control in that list, and what we can manage. But she took this one step further, encouraging people to write a scripture next to all our worries. Here are a few of my favourites: Joshua 1.6, where we are told to be bold and courageous, and 2 Chronicles 20.15 (NIV): 'Do not be afraid or discouraged . . . for the battle is not yours, but God's.'

Step 4: Find someone to share your fears with

Ideally, this should be someone with whom you can pray too! Someone with whom you can create a place where you can start to unpack what these fears really mean to you and the impact they are having on your mental health and well-being. Have someone who can help you embrace that pain and those fears and do it in a safe way where you feel supported and can lift everything to God together.

Prayer

God, at times trusting you feels impossible. At times it seems challenging, hard and as if I just don't know where to start. But I give you my fears. From the fear of . . . to the fear of . . . to . . . . Please help me to learn to trust you more, to be able to give all this to you. Please surround me with people with whom I can share these fears and from whom I can seek your support. Amen.

4

Free from lies

It was a warm September evening, and I was getting dolled up to go away for the weekend to see the latest boy I fancied. As I stood there, drying my hair in front of the mirror, I fixated on parts of my body I wanted to edit, lessen, maybe even cut out completely. Then my phone rang, the piercing ringtone cutting through the dangerous dialogue going on in my head: 'Come quickly; your mum has collapsed, and we can't get through to your dad . . .'

As soon as the words registered in my mind, I ran as fast as I could to where the stranger had told me to go, to find my mum and my little sister crying nearby. Before long, my dad arrived to take my sister home and I found myself in the back of the ambulance as we sped towards the hospital. Sitting there, I tried to push my emotions away. I boxed them out of view as I watched the paramedic put an oxygen mask on my mum. I pressed them further down as they transferred her to a bed in the hospital. I didn't want to feel them; I wanted to be strong, *fine*.

I wonder if you've ever found yourself feeling a similar way. Where things seem so out of control, too much to comprehend, that you just want to put a lid on everything you're feeling. Where you don't want to be a burden to anyone else so you just pretend you're fine. Sometimes that can be exacerbated when the reason we're feeling bad or low is that someone we know is going through something worrying and we feel the pressure to 'keep it together'. Thankfully, in this case, my mum did turn out to be all right, but I'll never forget that numbness of not allowing myself to feel what I was truly going through.

A study by the Mental Health Foundation, surveying 2,000 adults, found that the average adult will say 'I'm fine' 14 times a week, though just 19 per cent mean it.[8] And while this might seem like a 'fine' fib to tell, it is yet another lie that can keep us trapped inside our own heads, not able to let anyone into how we're doing. I for one know all too well that what can start out as a simple 'fib' can soon escalate until we're completely isolated by lies.

An untrustworthy friend

Although I had started having an unhealthy relationship with food as early as 13, by the age of 16 my illness was in full spate. What had started out as a 'friendship' (my anorexia being able to quell my anxieties with so-called control) had now moved past a 'romance' (something I was obsessed with) and into being a full-blown enemy. My eating disorder was beginning to ruin my life and, much worse, I didn't know how to stop it.

At first, I had managed to keep a lot of my unhealthy habits to do with eating in the dark, but people were starting to notice. Someone at the church youth group had mentioned that I needed to get help for my 'problem', whereas others simply kept reminding me to eat and keep warm. The problem was, my eating disorder was doing such a good job of convincing me that it had my best interests at heart that I couldn't detect the truth from the lies; I even felt that people were probably just telling me I needed to put on more weight because they were jealous. Then there was the fact that the truth of what people were saying made me feel scared and uncomfortable, whereas my eating disorder felt safe: it helped to numb everything I was feeling by distracting me with thinking about food, calories and exercise. It helped me to switch off from the day to day of life, taking me out of the reality of what was going on around me, and it was that that pulled me forward. I felt as if I just needed to do what she said with food and exercise and then I would be all right. She convinced me that if I listened more, did more of these behaviours, then at some point everything would work itself out.

Except I wasn't all right, and everyone knew it. And on some level, I knew it too. I still had a relationship with God and, although it was strained and confused, I still questioned his will for me. Did he care if I drank? What if I smoked? Was it even allowed? Was my eating disorder a sin? Was making myself sick after eating discounting me from his blessing? Should I tell anyone what was really going on? I prayed and prayed, but I didn't feel anything. Around this time, I wrote in my diary:

> I am so stressed out about my faith; it seems to have stopped and I have got all these questions which I have no answers to . . .

> I hate God and feel so unhappy. I know I need God in my life to feel content, but I want to focus more on weight at the moment . . .

> I felt really crap at church today. I wanted to get the gift of tongues, but I didn't . . .

My Christian friends were growing in their relationships with God, but I felt as if he was giving up on me. And so, in classic defence mode, I decided to give up on him instead, and very soon I stopped going to church altogether.

My weekend nights quickly turned into a repetitive cycle of drinking with my friends, feeling inadequate, getting home and then exercising into the early hours of the morning; my mind dominated by calorie counting to the point where it was hard to think about anything else. I was silently begging God to speak to me while making no room to listen to him. And the 'voice' of anorexia was getting louder until, by the time I was in the sixth form, there was no satisfying it. The one thing that had made me feel enough was now begging for more from me and, before long, I was becoming ever more noticeably unwell.

I didn't want to talk to anyone about what was going on and I didn't feel that anyone understood me. Plus, the lies in my head were so ingrained by now that I didn't even think I looked that thin. I lied my way through doctor's appointments, putting up a front, even when they said that they were referring me to Child and Adolescent Mental Health Services for a suspected eating disorder. I lied my way through my first appointment with the clinician, pretending I was listening to him telling me that I needed to put on weight when I was mentally working on my next excuse for missing dinner. Even in the next appointment, when he officially diagnosed me with anorexia, all I could think was that he was just jealous of me for finding this magical solution to life. And so, each time I returned for my weekly appointment, I hid my true feelings and pretended I was fine; I was getting good at it.

For the following six months, I worked out in secret, moving food around my plate during each evening meal to make it look as if I was eating more than I was. Though I wasn't convinced that I had anorexia, I knew that something was making me really unhappy. But I wasn't able to talk about it; it was easier just to be 'fine'. That was, until I couldn't hide it any more. My heart began to fail, and very soon I was admitted to a mental health hospital.[9]

One of the nurses showed me to my room and then sat down with me to talk me through my care plan and schedule. The whole day was dictated by food and rest, and I knew I had to find a way to get out of there. I was ushered into morning 'snack time' and a nurse sat with me while I pretended to take sips of the protein shake she was giving to me, sweat dripping down my back the entire time as my brain tried to comprehend how I had ended up here at the age of 17. Next, I was taken back to bed and told to rest. I curled up in a ball, my whole body aching as I ran my hand over it, wondering what was wrong with it. The next day came with the same regimented structure: up at 7 a.m. and weighed, breakfast at 8 a.m., morning snack at 11 a.m., lunch at 12.30 p.m., afternoon snack at 4 p.m., dinner at 6 p.m. and an evening snack at 8 p.m., but one visit was about to break the monotony. That evening, Emma, one of the nurses, came in. She laid a large piece of brown paper on the floor and asked me to draw myself and I did, drawing the ins and outs of my body, my arms and my stomach, all the while wondering how I was going to get out of this place and begin working on making myself thinner. After I had drawn myself, Emma asked me to lie down on the same piece of paper and, taking a different-coloured pen, she traced around me. Then we stood back to look at the images: what I thought I looked like and what my shape actually was. The images were so, *so* different. I didn't know what to say. I stood there staring down at them, trying to work out if what I was seeing was real. It was in that moment that I realized that maybe the view I had of myself and my body in my mind wasn't actually the truth. Maybe there *was* something the matter with me.

How do we loosen the stranglehold of lies?

How did I end up in this position? It's a question many of us will have asked ourselves from time to time – and not just those who have a complicated relationship with food. Our mental health can deteriorate slowly, like mine, or seemingly all at once; it can be circumstantial or it can feel completely out of the blue. The important thing is to surround oneself with people who will be able to recognize whether 'fine' really means 'fine'. In my case, it took me a lot longer than my loved ones to realize I needed support. But, as

Rachel Hughes of Gas Street Church explained to me, sometimes even the best support structure can't protect you from seasons of low mental health and well-being and it's important to know that God is with us through these times, whether we notice him or not.

'I was so blessed with the parenting and the upbringing I had, growing up in a safe and secure family,' Rachel shared with me. 'But when I hit my early teens, I had this realization that I didn't fit the "mould". There is such a strong narrative in society about what it is to be beautiful, but whatever that standard is, I knew I didn't live up to it. I felt ugly most of the time. I would look at my peers and feel this sense of insignificance and of just not being enough. At the same time, I discovered boys and I desperately wanted to be attractive to the opposite sex; it is a rite of passage in so many ways, but it felt very intense at the time. There were times when I hated the way I looked, and I would be sitting with such a sense of disappointment at this, and, coupled with the desire to be attractive to the opposite sex, it became a dangerous cycle for me.'

'When I won guys over, it fed this desperation in me to be noticed and worthy of love,' Rachel went on. 'I felt that if you didn't look right, then what hope was there? At university, the whole desire to be attractive and liked was such a big part of my life. I made choices about relationships and sex that I look back on now and think are reflective of someone with low self-worth. Around this time, I had walked away from God but never stopped believing in him, and so I began living this double life that I hated, and by the time I was in my early twenties I felt really empty on the inside but carried on hiding this from everyone around me.'

'I knew there was another way to live, and I longed for that,' Rachel added, reminding me of all the times I had felt the same way. 'I prayed a prayer and cried my heart out to God, and received this sense of his presence. After that I messed up a lot, but gradually began to learn what it really meant to live in the love of God and how to live as a follower of Jesus – and to realize it isn't cringe-worthy to be a Christian. But the reality is, I still have to come back to the truth that I am a daughter of the king, that I don't need to live up to cultural expectations.'

Rachel continued: 'It is so important that I spend time in God's presence, and this is a real game changer for me. The enemy tries to stop us from doing this, but it is about being disciplined in prior-itizing time with God and allowing God to shape our thinking. The next thing is about being aware of what we look at and watch! So many of us, me included, can spend hours scrolling on social media, constantly comparing our lives with the lives of others. I used to be so drawn to trashy magazines and, whether you are comparing or judging, both are bad! This is something I have to be really mindful of, even now.'

This was something that I knew was crucial for me, and may be for you too. We live in a society where there is this fixation with social media, with constantly parading our best selves. And although we all know that what we see on social media isn't the reality, so often when we are scrolling we aren't able to interrupt any sort of narra-tive about this! For me this also extends to not looking at social media when I am having a bad day but steering clear of it, as those moments tend to be when my brain self-destructs in a much more critical way.

The power of God's presence also rang through the story of another person I interviewed for this book, Hallie Heeg, who is the founder of WeRise, an international eating disorder, addiction, substance abuse and mental health organization helping individuals, families and professionals get the help and recovery support they need.

I first met Hallie when she spoke at an eating disorder support group I was running. She had this confidence about her, this glow, and she spoke with such conviction as she shared her story. Hallie grew up in the States as a pastor's child and the eldest of four, often struggling to feel heard and noticed. Her dad spent his time going backwards and forwards between what felt like two families, the church and theirs, and she sensed that she couldn't talk about how she truly felt, as she was viewed as living in this 'glass house' where the rest of the congregation was looking in.

'When I was about eight years old, I got a pair of glasses and a boy called me a "f**king four-eyes b**ch", and it was then that I began to feel self-conscious, noticing cliques forming, the more popular groups, and how I did or didn't fit into them. I moved schools when I was 13 years old and began to feel seen and heard, but as high school began the bullying started. I felt afraid, fearful and so jealous. I ended up going to my parents and sharing this with them, but their solution was to "pray more". I wanted someone to listen, to affirm me, but I felt so unheard and realized then that I had to find a way to cope with it all.'

Hallie continued: 'I developed bulimia as a coping mechanism. Every time I purged, I felt safe; it gave me control and got rid of those emotions that I didn't want to feel. Over the next few years, I started taking diet pills, drinking and exercising more. But instead of dealing with what I was going through, I focused my attention on others. On a random Sunday, I decided to go to church, and I signed up for the Rock Recovery Group, which was a 12-step Bible Recovery Programme. Over the next few months I gradually began to feel heard, and I loved the honesty and the openness. But over the next few years I had a huge amount of work that still needed to be done to manage my behaviours. It was like a Whack-a-Mole game; the alcohol stopped and the eating disorder popped up; the eating disorder went down and I looked to relationships to manage my emotions, and so on.'

'The greatest gift I could give myself was my own personal development,' Hallie explained further. 'I needed to start taking care of myself and learn how to love myself. Sharing my struggles was not a weak thing to do. At times we will get this wrong, but it isn't about being right all the time; it is about being in the world. I spent so much of my life not feeling enough, hating myself and not loving myself, but this began to shift. It didn't happen overnight, but over the next few years things began to change, and five or six years on I was starting to love myself and then, another year on, I started to know I was enough. I was able to move on from all those lies that had been dictated over my life and had held me back for too long.'

Moving on from the lies

I drew so much comfort from listening to Rachel Hughes and Hallie Heeg share their stories, as both had found a way to bring God into their situations to expose the lies under which they were living. Simply put, lies are the opposite of truth, so it is perhaps not that surprising that the Bible – a book that tells us that Jesus is the 'way and the truth and the life' (John 14.6, NIV) – also has a lot to say about lies and how we can combat their power in our lives.

To return to a scripture we looked at when considering shame, Genesis 3.1–6 (NIV) says:

Now the serpent was more crafty than any of the wild animals the LORD God had made. He said to the woman, 'Did God really say, "You must not eat from any tree in the garden"?' The woman said to the serpent, 'We may eat fruit from the trees in the garden, but God did say, "You must not eat fruit from the tree that is in the middle of the garden, and you must not touch it, or you will die."' 'You will not certainly die,' the serpent said to the woman. 'For God knows that when you eat from it your eyes will be opened, and you will be like God, knowing good and evil.' When the woman saw that the fruit of the tree was good for food and pleasing to the eye, and also desirable for gaining wisdom, she took some and ate it. She also gave some to her husband, who was with her, and he ate it.

We've already seen how this story plays out, with Jesus putting everything right through his sacrifice on the cross. And yet I want us to look more closely at the *way* the devil lied. He was crafty. He didn't lie outright; instead, he sowed seeds of doubts, spinning half-truths that sounded plausible. The lies that the devil tells us are often hard to spot because they dress themselves up in truth; they sound plausible. With the media constantly telling us we'll feel great if we lose that extra weight, or content when we meet and marry a romantic partner, or successful when we get that next promotion, is it any wonder that we can become obsessed with achieving these goals?

I was never explicitly *told* I wasn't enough, and there was no clear evidence for it. And yet I picked up on half-conversations, inferences from things people in my life did and didn't do, until I started to tell myself lie after lie. From this vantage point, any disappointments or hurts then seemed as if they were just reinforcing the evidence that had been planted all those years before. Perhaps you spend your time looking at social media and you accept the illusion that life is so much better for everyone else, or perhaps you grew up in a home where you were the shadow of someone else and you could never get to where you wanted to be, so you found a way to feel good enough? But the lie you were told led to another, and another, and another, and before you knew it you were ruminating over all the lies and beginning to let them win.

Each day we are faced with a barrage of messages, lies we have to deal with, and although we might tell ourselves we don't believe them, subconsciously this stuff affects us, so it is vital that we are mindful of it. John 10.10 says: 'The thief comes only to steal and kill and destroy' and we see this in every lie that we are told. But this scripture then goes on to say: 'I have come that they may have life, and have it to the full.' Whether we sense his presence or not, we can be sure that God is with us and for us. As we read in Psalm 145.18 (HCSB): 'The Lord is near all who call out to Him, all who call out to Him with integrity.' For both Rachel and Hallie, there came a point when they could run away from God no longer and instead turned all their anxieties and struggles with their mental health towards him, creating space for him to speak.

The good news is that God will listen to us, even when we don't know what to say. God has given us the gift of the Holy Spirit and look how this is described in John 14.15–31 (NIV): 'And I will ask the Father, and he will give you another advocate to help you and be with you forever – the Spirit of truth.' The Spirit of truth is working alongside us to expose the lies and this advocate will work within us even when we're lost for words: 'the Spirit helps us in our weakness. We do not know what we ought to pray for, but the Spirit himself intercedes for us through wordless groans' (Romans 8.26, NIV).

For Ruth Kirkland, a children's ministry worker based in Hertfordshire, it was creating space for the Holy Spirit to speak that first helped her filter through the truth and lies in her life. 'I had been a Christian for some time when I had a revelation of how Jesus had died for me and just how much he loved me. For the first 14 years of my faith journey, I had known I was very loved, precious and valuable to God, but my faith also felt "dry" and very one-sided. Then I was baptized by the Holy Spirit and suddenly I was filled with a love for God that I hadn't experienced before, and my relationship with him really started to develop and grow deeper. Not only did I pray to God, but I also gradually began to hear from him in many different ways. Life feels like an adventure, and I know God has got me, even in the tough times! God continues to change me, free me, empower me and grow me,' Ruth continues. 'I know that when this life is over, I will be with Jesus for ever. I find that surrender is something that I come back to again and again. Filling myself with the truth of who God is, and who he says I am, is so important: then I find myself less fearful and more able to trust in an almighty and all-powerful and wise God who also loves me unconditionally and more deeply than I will ever understand or know. I read the Bible, listen to truth-filled worship songs, remind myself of what God has done in my past and of his faithfulness; I listen to and read other people's testimonies; I spend time with God; I ask others to pray for me and to help me to understand the lies that I am believing so I can be freed from them with God's help.'

As well as making time to spend with God, in the same way we would with a friend, it is also important to *protect* this time. The same scripture we looked at earlier, John 14.15–31 (NIV), goes on to say: 'The world cannot accept [the Holy Spirit] because it neither sees him nor knows him. But you know him, for he lives with you and will be in you'. Elsewhere, in Matthew 13 (NIV), Jesus tells the parable of the sower. After sharing the story where the seed (which represents the message about the kingdom of God) is scattered on the ground and announcing that some seeds will thrive and others won't survive, Jesus goes on to explain what it means in verse 19:

> When anyone hears the message about the kingdom and does not understand it, the evil one comes and snatches away what

was sown in their heart. This is the seed sown along the path. The seed falling on rocky ground refers to someone who hears the word and at once receives it with joy. But since they have no root, they last only a short time. When trouble or persecution comes because of the word, they quickly fall away. The seed falling among the thorns refers to someone who hears the word, but the worries of this life and the deceitfulness of wealth choke the word, making it unfruitful. But the seed falling on good soil refers to someone who hears the word and understands it. This is the one who produces a crop, yielding a hundred, sixty or thirty times what was sown.

Once we hear the Word of God, we have to protect this truth in our lives. As well as guarding our time with God, we must also be mindful of the other influences and voices we let into our minds. For Rachel Hughes, who like me has struggled with trying to control her weight, this mindfulness of what information she fills her mind with extends to going through seasons of not weighing herself. In her case, this involved completely refraining from weighing herself for three years in order to get to a place where she was able to have a better relationship with the scales. For others, it will be a decision to limit the time you spend on social media or not to read trashy magazines if they always leave you feeling lower in mood. Perhaps the key question each of us needs to ask is, what purpose is 'this' serving in my life? In the depths of my eating disorder, weighing myself felt like a good way of dictating whether I was good enough. My weight gave me the self-worth that I wasn't able to get from myself or others. If I had lost weight I would feel (momentarily) worthy, whereas if I had gained any, I would feel that I was failing. Because of these behaviours and thoughts, I began to get much of my self-worth from that number on the scales. It is so important for us to take the time to recognize what we're taking into our minds, why we are doing it and what the impact is when we do it. And yet we should not feel bad every time we do these things, sacrificing social media and trashy magazines out of tired obligation, but instead look to the joy it is to spend time with Jesus.

'Young people are listening to different voices,' said Hannah Williams, who works as a church consultant, in particular helping churches with their youth ministries. 'Children listen predominantly to their parents' voices but when they become teenagers this often changes.' Hannah then went on to say that teenagers explore other voices that they want to listen to, whether it is media, celebrities or the church. 'For me, it is about helping young people to hear the voice of God and to understand what God is saying about them. I learned to listen to God as a teenager and to seek him when I was having those harder moments, and to centre my life on his truth.'

Practical steps

Step 1: Begin to spend time with God

As you've seen above, I came to a point where my mental health condition drowned out the voice of God and even my need for him. If this has happened to you, please have grace for yourself. Even so, we have seen so much evidence in this chapter that simply sitting with God and allowing him space to work can change everything. Can you challenge yourself to spend even five minutes in silence before God today, concentrating on simply *being* rather that looking for answers or outcomes? Remember, the Spirit can lift your groans for you!

Step 2: Be mindful of what you are flooding your brain with . . .

We live in a noisy society, where there are many voices vying for our attention. Take social media, for example, something that is full of such dangerous content and comparison-rife material. Taking time to curate what we look at so we are aware of what we are feeding our minds with is so important: does it make you feel good? Does it bring you closer to God? Maybe you even need to limit your time on there or take a break from social media completely, particularly if you are tired, or not having a good day.

Step 3: Make a distinction between fact and opinion

When someone has declared something about you, whether advertising or the media or a relative or friend, take the time to ask yourself where this voice is coming from and what the motive is behind it, and invite God to help you filter facts from opinions – in these moments I sometimes ask myself 'Did God really say this?' and it helps to get rid of the untruths!

Prayer

Dear God, I know there are times when I feel I am failing, times when life seems relentless and I don't really feel good enough. Please help me in these moments to learn how to focus on you. Please help me to flood myself with truth from you and not to let the lies pull me back. Amen.

5

Free from wounds

Life in hospital carried on, the days turning into weeks and the weeks into months until I had been there almost an entire year. At moments I just wanted it to stop, but somehow I kept moving forward, motivated by life on the other side of recovery; life had felt as if it had been on pause for the last year and I knew I wanted to make up for lost time.

Once I was out of hospital, I went straight to the University of Birmingham. Studying with mental health issues had its own challenges, but I kept my head in the game by focusing on my meal plan and trying to be honest with my family about what was happening. Each day felt like a step forward in my recovery and over time things began to seem much easier to navigate. Graduating three years later, I bumbled between jobs and lived in Asia for a year until a relapse in 2016 led me to grow tired of the support systems for mental illness (or lack thereof) and I decided that I needed to speak up in order to help others. At the end of 2016, I left my job and decided I was going to make it my full-time mission to campaign for better treatment of mental illness, pushing for an end to the injustices people face. And yet, despite making strides in my recovery, deep inside I knew something was still holding me back.

Is there something in your past that you feel rears its head again and again, whether it be a memory or a negative thought pattern that you find hard to shake? For some, their past may act as a motivation to propel them forward, but for others it might make them feel like giving up. That nothing will change, leaving them with a whole load of anger and frustration. We see motivational quotes all over social media telling us that 'our past cannot define us' and to 'never look back', but there is something quite important and helpful in looking backwards. Looking backwards, and giving ourselves space to process things, helps resolve past hurts and also helps us to create a greater awareness of triggers in life. An article by Miriam Akhtar, author of *#What Is Post-Traumatic Growth?*, talks about the importance of having that space to unpack what is going on for someone. She emphasizes that humans construct stories to get meaning, and to create a new narrative. Whether we are going to see a therapist or a friend or journalling, it can help us move on from our past.[10] It sounds so simple in theory, doesn't it? Write something down, talk about an event to a friend and everything will be fine. But no matter how many self-help books or articles we read promising us a quick fix for moving on from the things that hold us back, the truth is that some of us just have to do the hard work of exposing our wounds, however painful that might feel, and revisiting them as many times as it takes for them to heal for good; plastering over something can only work for so long.

For me, one of these wounds was the sexual abuse I suffered as a teenager. The definition of abuse is: 'any action that intentionally harms or injures another person. In short, someone who purposefully harms another in any way is committing abuse.'[11] I pray that you have not experienced any abuse in your life, but if you have, there is nothing to be ashamed of and there is no wound so deep that God cannot heal it. But we do not need to suffer abuse to feel held back by memories of the past; perhaps there is a dream that you had that hasn't come to fruition, leaving you with a deep feeling of disappointment. Or maybe there is something hurtful someone said about you when you were younger that went right to the heart of your identity. Our past hurts don't have to be something that the world sees as 'huge'. As individuals we need to stop comparing our trauma and our history with those of others, as it often stops us reaching out for support. Trauma is defined in the dictionary as 'a deeply distressing or disturbing experience' and, unaddressed, it can have a real impact on our mental health and, in some situations, contribute to a person's developing a mental illness. Research also shows strong links between trauma and self-blame, where we blame ourselves for what happened to us or, in some cases, blame ourselves for not dealing better with what happened.[12] There is a great deal of evidence[13] out there from all over the world showing that, from an emotional, spiritual and physical point of view, talking things out and sharing what is going on rather than maintaining secrecy helps reduce the impact the event has had on us.[14]

Revisiting old wounds

I had kept quiet for so long about what had happened to me, but it still haunted me. Every night when I got into bed, even when I was on trains travelling around the country to speak to schools about eating disorders and run workshops on mental health, I was afraid of seeing his piercing eyes penetrate through my entire body again. I continued to keep a close eye on him, gaining as much information as I could from his Facebook page; once again, I felt myself trying to keep a sense of control over the situation. I worried about it happening again; I worried about what he might do to others. And I knew now that I needed to speak up to gain more freedom from this part of my life and find a way to move on from it.

It was a hot morning when I arrived at the police station, full of anxiety about what people would say, what they might think, when I told them what I was about to tell them. I knew at any point I could turn round and back out; after all, I'd not reported the incidents for 15 years; was revisiting this really going to help anyone? Still,

I carried on walking into the station and they showed me where I would be sitting for the next few hours, reliving something that had been boxed up for so long. I sat down on the sofa in the hot, sticky room as someone explained that my interview would be filmed by someone watching it from another room. My mind was racing with questions: what if I couldn't do this? What if I froze up? Was my skirt riding up my leg? Would they think I was 'easy'? Why hadn't I put on tights? I grabbed my yellow mac that I had thrown down next to me and pulled it over myself, shrinking back into the seat as I stated my name and date of birth and regressed to my teenage self.

As the months passed after that first disclosure to the police, all I could do was wait. The police began to question my family, old boyfriends, close friends; they searched my mum's house for old diaries and my hospital notes were torn apart. I remember their calling me back into the station to ask follow-up questions that I struggled to answer: why didn't your mum like him? What did he get out of touching you? Did you say 'no' to him then? How about this time? How about that time? . . . I began to clam up: no, I didn't say no every time; I was afraid to. But just because I wasn't saying no, it didn't mean I was saying yes. The more they questioned me, the more I questioned myself: had I allowed this to happen? Had it been my fault? I lay there so many evenings doubting whether I had made the right decision by reporting it. I knew the statistics on successful prosecutions for sexual abuse were as low as in 2005, 5.7 per cent,[15] but over the last few years they have hit a new record low.[16] The added complication in my case was that I had left it so many years before coming forward, which I knew meant that it might be harder to prosecute because of the lack of visible evidence. And added to all the doubt about whether I would be believed or not, whether they would acknowledge that he had messed up my life, I was struggling with feeling guilty about ruining his. The truth is, it was hard coming forward, but I knew it was important for me to do it. I would always encourage others to report abuse but really believe it is up to each individual to work out whether or not they want to do so. In my case, it helped bring closure and gave me a space to be heard. Although I didn't have the best experience, I was inspired by the fact that individuals such as MP Jess Phillips, who constantly shines a light on the injustices that people face in reporting sexual abuse cases, give me hope that things can change for the better.

As I waited for news from the police, I found ways to distract myself with work. I campaigned constantly, travelling all over the country to speak in schools and thriving on the busy days as it meant I didn't have to deal with any emotions. I fixated on helping others because it gave me a real sense of purpose. Looking back, I can see some of my old unhealthy coping mechanisms trying to suck me back in. I had shared more of my story, and I had absolutely no control over how the people I had trusted with this would respond. Having by now turned my back on God, I found myself wanting to reach out to him again. It wasn't so much a choice, but a desperate cry from my heart to his. As the author and activist Glennon Doyle says in her book *Untamed*, I suppose 'there was always part of church in me'.[17] One night, I found myself crying out to God, pacing around my flat as I shouted angry prayers. Once again, I was spilling my heart out, but I had no control over the response: if God existed, why had this happened? If God loved me, why didn't he take away this hurt?

And it wasn't just God I started to share with. I always talked in my mental health workshops about the importance of opening up and I knew I had to start taking my own advice. So, over the next few months, I plucked up every ounce of courage left in me and gradually began to open up to those closest to me about what I was going through. As I started to share, a weight began to be lifted and I was so encouraged by the responses. I was fortunate to find that I had a supportive network around me, which gave me the confidence to be honest with those people close to me. It can feel really scary talking about things and I certainly don't want to play that down, especially if you don't feel you have a similarly supportive network around you, but I want to encourage you to start small: maybe share a bit of information with someone very close to you first, and then gradually over time you can start to explore and open up more.

During this time, I was also starting to notice that I was having more and more encounters with people who believed in God. As the case proceeded further and the investigator was getting ready to present the evidence to the Crown Prosecution Service (CPS), I met this lovely woman called Ruth when I was visiting a school one day. She was so confident in who she was, who God made her to be, and her openness and love for God and others shone through when she spoke. Despite my complicated relationship with God, I found myself becoming increasingly drawn to her. Then I met Sean Fletcher, who had agreed to come to Downing Street with me as part of the #DumpTheScales campaign in April 2019. Back then I had no idea he was a Christian, but, as I began to explore what faith was, he took the time to share worship songs with me. I felt particularly struck by Sean, who had talked publicly in the past about his own family's experience with mental health, and I was fascinated by how he still believed in God after so much had happened. Added to that, I began to communicate with my godmother Sarah, with whom I had lost touch years before; I messaged her out of the blue and she replied, eager to build a relationship with me and sharing what she had been doing. Even when I felt so down, so far from God, it seemed that he was waiting for me to turn to him again, putting people in my life to draw me back to him.

I decided to start praying daily again, reasoning that if I prayed enough God would *have* to respond. But, after two weeks of praying the same prayers, bargaining with God for him to fix everything, I found out that my court case had fallen through because there wasn't enough evidence. It had come down to my word against his, and because they thought he was no longer a threat, they didn't see the need to carry on with it. I was left feeling further from God than ever. Why did everything hurt so much? Why had my attempts to speak up come to nothing? The problem was, in praying for a specific outcome, expecting God to respond to my wishes like some kind of genie, I didn't realize the many ways in which he was already healing me and the powerful way he was going to move next.

My seemingly random encounters with God-lovers had started to chip away at my defences but, in the wake of my court case being thrown out, my walls were firmly back up. That was until a stranger at Highbury and Islington Station witnessed them come crashing back down. Sitting there, waiting for my train home, I felt lower than I had for a very long time. I had done the hard work of hospital, the hard work of healing, the hard work of opening myself up, and for what? Just to feel more pain than I had before? A few people stopped to ask whether I was all right, but a sharp 'I'm fine' turned them away. Not this one man, however. Instead, he sat with me for 45 minutes, telling me all about his faith, about how his love and trust in God kept him going: a love and trust in a God whom I had been trying my best to push away. As the stranger disappeared into the crowd, his words stayed with me; he had had this presence about him that I couldn't shake. I got home that evening and immediately messaged my godmother and Ruth, telling them about the rather strange encounter I had had. Ruth replied later that evening, telling me she felt nudged to pray for me and also suggesting I attend a service at HTB Church. And so, the following weekend, I went. I was scared, but curious about why all these people kept turning to God in prayer and praise. Sitting there by myself, I looked around the building trying to take in everything in it. I had positioned myself three rows from the back, three seats in from a huge stone pillar, calculating it to be the perfect place to sit if you wanted no one to talk to you. Still, I watched everyone around me closely as they sang songs of worship and prayed along with the preacher, longing to work out what was going on for them, why they all looked so peaceful. I wanted what they had but it seemed so out of reach. I had worked for it, bargained for it, wrestled for it, but now I had no energy to fight. I had to let go. But I was soon about to learn that it's in our surrender that God can really get to work; that when God felt 'out of reach', he was reaching out to me, willing to make me whole.

Opening up to let God in

Looking back at this time in my life, I can see why I found it so difficult. On the one hand, I knew I needed to open up in order to find more freedom from my need for control, and yet, as I shared, I had zero control over the response of the recipient, whether that be the police, the people around me, or God. My abuse and the subsequent deterioration of my mental health had started at a church youth group and yet, years later, God was calling me back to his community of believers, the Church, the very place by which I had felt so let down.

I sat down with Mary Thorne, a primary school adviser for the London Diocesan Board for Schools, in what was another of those so-called chance encounters that I had around this time. Mary had invited me to speak at a head teachers' conference in Poole, about eating disorders and what schools can do to support people. As we spoke together, she shared with me: 'I had always gone to church, and this had shaped so much of who I was; I felt unconditionally loved by my family and knew I was a child of God. But this all became problematic when I was becoming aware of my own sexuality and that I was gay. I was anxious about how the Church would respond to this. I was getting more and more unsure about how I could remain a member of the Church and be gay at the same time.' Mary's scenario might have been very different from my own, but I could relate to the fact that the Church, a community where Mary was told she should be safe, had become somewhere that she doubted would accept her and love her as she was. It was somewhere that wasn't a source of healing but rather one of hurt. So how did she get through this? How does she still remain faithful to the Church today?

Quoting Mary herself again: 'After much thought, I knew that I had to find a way to stay in the Church so I could help shape its attitude towards gay people and make it a more loving and accepting place. For me, it is about separating the notion of the Church as an institution from the faith it attempts to proclaim. The first thing I did was realize that the Church (while incredibly important) does not define the identity of God. To me, God is a God of love, revealed in Jesus. That has not changed. The great commandments are to love God and love your neighbour, and that's what we must continue to do as we meet people where they are. The institution sometimes gets this wrong and can be judgemental or critical and in some cases even actually hurt people. We must somehow learn to live with hurtful events that have happened in the past as well as try to understand the Church's perspective. I have navigated this whole area by being surrounded by empathetic people in the Church and by being with people who have helped me understand who God is. Something that really helps me in these moments is to continue to find a way to be authentic. I am open to listening when people disagree with me, whether that's about my own sexuality or about the hurt the Church may cause. Through all these discussions, I attempt to remain respectful. If an individual church isn't able to welcome me as I am, then I know it isn't the place for me.'

As I listened to Mary, I remembered all over again how I had often confused my relationship with God with my relationship with the Church and what happened within it. The Church is something that the Bible tells us is vitally important to God and his purposes in the world, but it is also formed of human beings, many of whom have been broken and hurt themselves. I'm not sure if you've ever heard the phrase 'Hurt people hurt people', but this seems apt in both my own and Mary's case. Still, God is bigger than the Church as an institution, and the Church in the Bible is painted, at its very simplest, as a community of believers – not a building, or traditions, or anything else human-made that we sometimes let become bigger than God himself. When I think back on my adolescence, I can see that there were many times when I felt let down by those at church, or those in authority, and how I let this muddle my views of God, but this is what the enemy wants. He wants us to get stuck in our past, stuck in the wounds, and stop believing that God can save us. And, as Mary shared with me, as time trickles by, this lie can take on even more weight; in her own words: 'It is so hard to understand why God does and doesn't take away those wounds and heal people straight away. When we look at the Gospels, there are so many encounters where Jesus healed people. For me, healing is a process. The problem is, in our society we see that some people have been healed, so we start comparing. The truth is that healing doesn't always look how we expect it to. Someone may not be healed from a specific wound immediately, but it could be a continuous process of healing. I strongly believe that full healing will happen when we die, when we meet Christ in eternity. Resilience and persistence are the keys! One has to accept, however, that sometimes you will be in a real desert place. I was in this place when I was a student for a long period of time. I felt God wasn't there. But what we do in those situations is so important. If we trust that faith will return, membership of the Church can help and sustain us in the desert. In my case, making sure that I kept going each week proved vital even when I didn't want to, along with not losing sight of hope. I think that having had a previous encounter with Christ helped, and for me this happened when I was 14. I have never doubted God's existence. Having moments of profound questioning and feeling frustrated and angry – all that is allowed. It is about being real. We don't have to be on a high all the time or have all the answers. It might be about living in the fog of doubt a lot of the time. We need to move away from absolutes and be reconciled to living in the grey area much of the time.'

Mary reminded me that: 'Christianity is not about the dos and don'ts. It is about accepting that Jesus is God. Christian theology is about a relationship with God. It is hard at times to live in a loving relationship with him. But if bad things happen, it is not because God is punishing us. And although we cannot understand why some people are well and others are not – and I can't answer this question – I believe God will keep working things out with us. What I also believe is that he will only give us as much as we can cope with. That might seem ridiculous, but if we believe we are in the palm of his hands, he will help us through it. For me, it is about being aware of all that surrounds us and knowing God can speak to us through a range of means and experiences.'

Wounds and the Word

When it comes to our mental well-being and experiencing periods of poor mental health, it is so important to remember that these feelings will pass and, more than this, that God can meet us right in the middle of them. In our interview, Mary pointed to the fact that we can *know* that Jesus has the power to heal. The Bible is full of evidence of Jesus doing just this, from turning water into wine in John 2.1–11 (NIV) to raising Lazarus from the dead in John 11.1–46. From physical healings to miracles of provision, such as the feeding of at least five thousand people with five loaves of bread and two fish in Matthew 14.15, we see time and time again that Jesus has the power to heal completely and immediately. We can also see that Jesus has the power to bring peace, literally and metaphorically. In Matthew 8.23–27 (NIV) we read how Jesus stilled the storm:

> Then he got into the boat and his disciples followed him. Suddenly a furious storm came up on the lake, so that the waves swept over the boat. But Jesus was sleeping. The disciples went and woke him, saying 'Lord, save us! We're going to drown!' He replied, 'You of little faith, why are you so afraid?' Then he got up and rebuked the winds and the waves, and it was completely calm. The men were amazed and asked, 'What kind of man is this? Even the winds and the waves obey him!'

How amazing it is to know that we can follow a God with the power to still the storm. But also how confusing, when we're crying out for help and find ourselves feeling that Jesus may just be sleeping on the job.

First, it's important to remember that God's timing isn't our timing. As we've already seen, we often want things to change quickly – particularly when we feel we're in the middle of a storm – but we once again see much evidence in the Bible of God's timing and agenda being very different from our own. Proverbs 3:5–6 (NIV) encourages us to 'trust in the Lord with all your heart and lean not on your own understanding' and in 2 Peter 3.8–9 (NIV) we read:

> But do not forget this one thing, dear friends: with the Lord a day is like a thousand years, and a thousand years are like a day. The Lord is not slow in keeping his promise, as some understand slowness. Instead he is patient with you, not wanting anyone to perish, but everyone to come to repentance.

We see in this scripture that often God wants to use the time in between hearing our prayers and healing us to do something different within us, in this case bringing people closer to him so that they can know him intimately. As Ecclesiastes 3:1 confirms, 'there is a time for everything, and a season for every activity under the heavens', including times of sadness and lament through which God can still work.

When we find ourselves in seasons that feel sticky and we can't see a way out of them, Mary's words were so apt when she told me: 'Resilience and persistence are the keys!' We need to find the resilience it takes to keep coming back to God, choosing to be honest with him even when it hurts, as for example in Habakkuk 1 (NIV), where we read: 'How long, LORD, must I call for help, but you do not listen? Or cry out to you, "Violence!" but you do not come to save?' Taking our fears and doubts to God means we no longer need to be burdened with them all by ourselves. I want you to take another moment to be honest with God: what is holding you back? What is stopping you from letting go of that wound? Have you taken the time to tell God what you are *really* thinking and feeling about it? Let it all out, be honest, share those thoughts, that thinking, those frustrations. It might feel uncomfortable, but it will help.

Some of you may be thinking: what's the point? I've been honest in the past with God, done all this before, but nothing ever changes. I've had all these feelings too but the Bible yet again gives us a great example of the fact that persistence in prayer can truly change things. In Joshua 6 we read the story of the walls of Jericho. We learn how Joshua was commanded to walk around the city walls seven times, and the seventh time, the walls fell down. I used to think this was a bit ridiculous. If God is so powerful, surely he could have knocked those walls down straight away, yet he chose not to. Sometimes in our lives things happen and we simply cannot understand why, but we have to keep going; we have to keep circling round that one thing! I have had so many walls of Jericho, from my recovery to some of my campaigning work (you should see my face when I get emails from ministers who think eating disorder services are fully funded); I had to keep circling those walls, to keep showing up day in, day out, even if at points the easier thing to do would have been to stay in bed. This story is one of my favourite stories in the Bible, because it really shows, as Mary said earlier in this chapter, that persistence is the key! It also encourages us to look for where God is working as we are walking: maybe he wants us to learn more about him, his character, his love. If God answered immediately, would we lean on him more or turn him into a holy slot machine?

I may have been praying for my court case to be successful, finally to get justice in relation to my sexual abuse, but God answered my prayers in a different way. He drew me closer to him by placing key people in my life during this time. As I was calling out to him in desperation, God was perfectly positioning these people in my life, in a way that he knew would speak to me and ultimately lead me back into the arms of his community of believers. As Mary shared in our chat, despite the pain and confusion being a member of a church had caused her in the past: 'Being a member of the Church helps . . . and not losing sight of the hope that it will end.' Supported by those who love Jesus and know how to point us towards him, we can hold on to the promise of Jeremiah 29.11–12 (NIV) together:

> For I know the plans I have for you, declares the LORD, plans to prosper you and not to harm you, plans to give you hope and a future. Then you will call on me and come and pray to me, and I will listen to you.

Practical steps

Step 1: Identify old wounds and open yourself up

Allow yourself to feel the pain, whether that is in therapy, when talking to people or in your prayer time, and allow God to gently put his hand on the hurting places that he wants to heal.

Step 2: Build a support structure of hope around yourself

Looking back on this time in my life, I know God was drawing me back into a church community. For you this might involve going to a big church or simply meeting with a trusted friend to pray. Either way, begin to open up to people who can point you to God.

Step 3: Just keep walking

As we have seen, resilience and persistence are essential. Find things that build your resilience – whether that's time with friends or reading the Bible or listening to worship music – and then keep coming back to God in prayer. Sometimes it is truly about taking another walk around that Jericho wall, getting up and taking another step, reminding yourself that God is faithful and that he is already working in you and through you, whether you see it or not.

Prayer

Lord, these wounds feel deep; they feel heavy and unfair in places. But I am choosing to walk in faith, choosing to trust even when I don't understand the way. Please help me to keep taking one step forward, to keep circling those walls, and help me to remain strong. Amen.

6

Free to forgive

'The only way to get to heaven is to repent of your sin!' The words bellowed through the man's speakers on the edge of Oxford Circus tube station. I scuttled past, keeping my head down, as someone thrust a pamphlet into my hands. I shoved it into my bag, making my way through the crowds as I commenced my walk to Waterloo Station. As I waited to cross the road by Waterloo Bridge, my eyes caught a sign on a bus that asked: 'Is there more to life than this?' with a huge red question mark next to it. This question was harder to ignore.

As I tried to go about my day the question niggled me, reminding me of all the other questions that I had asked and felt were left unanswered. Though the threatening bellow of 'sin' made me want to hide, the open-ended question on the bus made me want to find out more. I'm not sure what *you* think about when you hear words like 'sin' or 'redemption'. If you are anything like me, they probably make you feel slightly unsettled and a bit unnerved. I had drifted so far away from God all those years ago that these words barely crossed my mind and that was how I liked it . . . or so I *thought*.

'Forgiveness' can evoke different things for different people; we have probably all heard people say, 'I'll never forgive them' and mean it, and for some the idea of forgiving someone who has caused them pain seems like 'letting them off the hook'. And yet research has shown that the impact of forgiveness on our mental health and well-being is huge![18] Not only does forgiveness increase positive emotions but it also helps reduce negative ones, such as blame and anger, which if we're not careful can eat us up from the inside. Though the positive impacts of forgiveness are widely documented both inside and outside Christian circles, as followers of Jesus we can point to *why* forgiveness is a gift and know that there is a link between forgiving others and being forgiven ourselves. As we read in Matthew 6.14: 'For if you forgive other people when they sin against you, your heavenly Father will also forgive you.' But this doesn't make forgiving those who have hurt us any easier. As I was about to discover, 'letting go and letting God' can be challenging, threatening and downright messy.

A stumbling block in the road

'Is there more to life than this?' The sign I saw on the bus was for the Alpha Course, a course that is generally run through churches that I am sure some of you will be aware of. Perhaps a few months beforehand, I would have just ignored this question in the same way I had the perhaps less than helpful station evangelist, but after attending the HTB church service a handful of times, I was finding myself praying more regularly and becoming more and more intrigued. If I woke up feeling rubbish, I would pray – even if no one was there it felt good always to have somebody to talk to. Even so, I knew I was still carrying a huge amount of anger and confusion in the wake of my failed court case. I was feeling punished by my past and began longing to feel that peace that so many talked about in church, but I had no idea where to start. I spent hours googling and reading stories of people who had been healed, people who had found peace, people who were settled, and I knew I wanted to explore my faith further.

With much trepidation, I turned up for the first Alpha Course session at HTB. By now, I knew that it was a course held in countless churches across the globe, but at a big church like HTB I assumed I would be able to remain quite anonymous. As I approached the church, I could feel myself wanting to back away, but I had already told my godmother I was coming tonight and so forced myself to go inside. I was shocked to find the church filled with loud conversations, with what must have been hundreds of people sitting around in groups. I gazed around, feeling consumed by emotion, plastered on my 'game face' and found a chair. As people introduced themselves in our smaller discussion group, I concentrated on asking the others questions; I wasn't yet sure which side of myself I wanted to share with these strangers. I concentrated on my campaigning, not the painful reasons that had prompted it.

The Alpha session followed the same structure it would do each week. It began with a meal and catching up with your discussion group; then you watched a video for about 20 minutes and discussed this video in your group. As we discussed each topic – from who Jesus is to what evidence there is that he existed – I tried to keep everything together; I even ate my dinner on the way to the course so that the people there wouldn't know I'd ever had an eating disorder. It was all going well until the dreaded topic came up: *forgiveness*. As I sat there watching the video, hearing stories of how others had forgiven people for horrendous and hurtful acts, I felt the pressure mounting to finally forgive my abuser. But how could I? Even now, I was still having horrific nightmares about what he did to me. I knew on some level that forgiveness would be good for me, even if I wasn't a Christian. But did I really have the strength to let go?

Before long, the Alpha Weekend Away became a talking point; it was a chance to go deeper in our relationship with God and with the other people on the Course. It may not surprise you by now to learn that I didn't commit to the Weekend Away until just the week before. As the days turned into hours before we were due to go, I could feel the fear settling in. On the one hand, I wasn't sure I believed everything we were talking about. And, on the other, I knew I was secretly piling expectations on this weekend for something amazing to happen; I was looking for some kind of confirmation that God cared or daring to expect the instant healing for which I had been hoping for so long. I was so scared of what would happen if I gave control over to God, but mostly I think I was scared of what *might not* happen.

The first night of the weekend was hard; mealtimes were a minefield and I felt myself getting frustrated with God that it wasn't easier, but soon I found myself distracted by the talks and activities before heading back to my own room, relieved to have space to process things. The next day, we focused on what it meant to be 'filled with the Holy Spirit'. As I sat there praying, I felt my mind wander back to over a decade ago when I was at Christian youth festivals waiting for the Holy Spirit to fall, feeling as if he'd somehow missed me off the agenda, and making up what I had 'felt' just so I could be part of something. As I sat there reflecting on things, I kept remembering how I believed there was something wrong with me, which is why I couldn't feel what everyone else was feeling. Soon a friend offered to pray with me. I said I wasn't up to it. I felt angry with everyone. Angry with my abuser, angry with God, angry with myself. Even so, I stayed to listen as a handful of people shared prophecies they felt they had for the group. I remember one saying she sensed that someone had been rejected in the past, but God would never reject them. At that point everything became too much and I left the room. My friend caught up with me and we prayed and cried together. I still felt so much pain but felt seen – that she understood the wounds, scars and brokenness. That evening, I felt an incredible sense of gratefulness that God had put all these people around me and a hope that maybe I didn't have to have all my questions answered before I made a decision about what I believed. I could learn along the way, as we do in recovery from any mental illness. We step outside our comfort zones into a space of fear and uncertainty, which, although it feels scary, can also present us with some amazing opportunities. We so often think that we must look a certain way or be a certain type of person for God to fix us, but we don't have to. I had been so set on being completely perfect for God that I had lost sight of what a relationship was. And so, on the Sunday, as I stood there worshipping, I sensed a growing realization that God had been with me through my illness and throughout my life; I felt a sense of relief and peace but was still conscious of that nagging worry, fearful of how long these feelings would last. That weekend marked the start of my 'forgiving' God, forgiving myself and forgiving others, but, as I was about to find out, it was only the beginning.

Can God love me even when I am broken?

It wasn't until I realized that I didn't need to be 'fixed' for God to love me that my faith started to change. If we're struggling with mental health or a mental illness it can sometimes be hard not to see ourselves as too 'damaged' and get our health mixed up with the love and contentment for which God designed us. I was encouraged when speaking to Zeke Rink of Dreaming the Impossible to find that I was not alone in how I was feeling: 'None of us is perfect and as individuals we actually need to recognize that we are sinful. We won't find the answers in ourselves, but Jesus has the answers. He can give us hope. It is not a problem to recognize that we sin because there is a way forward: Jesus defeated sin and the death on the cross. He gave us this space to keep going back to him and asking for that forgiveness. We aren't meant to beat ourselves up for our sin but to recognize the sin and then recognize the Saviour before realizing who we are in him.'

I don't know about you, but to me this offer of forgiveness is such a gift – one that sometimes even sounds too good to be true. One worry that held me back from receiving this gift fully was the false idea that God was punishing me and withholding himself from me because of my abuse and eating disorder and the fact they were preventing me from living the 'best' possible Christian life that I could. This is something that editor, writer and model Tola Doll Fisher had to learn to unpack on her own journey towards healing in Christ.

'When I was 18 years old, I had an abortion,' Tola shared with me. 'I got married at 26 and then fell pregnant. I lost my baby shortly after her birth and soon hit this wilderness in my life. I thought for a long time that the reason I had lost my child was as a punishment for the abortion I had had. I felt so low and unsure how to cope with what was going on. I ended up doing what I could to numb the pain, drinking and partying all the time. I was still a Christian at this point and felt God telling me to stop and slow down. But I had no idea how to or what that would look like. So I ended up booking a ski season with a Christian organization. Getting away from the UK and having some space away from what was going on, I allowed myself to cry, to think, to rest. The ski season gave me a chance to reset. And on my return to England, I joined a new church and began to learn more about God and who he actually is.'

'I had to be honest, saying things like, "I don't think God is good; I think God is X, Y, Z",' Tola explained further. 'The only way for me to find forgiveness for myself and others was to accept where I was and then move on from that moment. I did the Redemption Course at a New Frontiers Church, which helped me process everything and learn more about God's nature. I read so many different stories in the Bible and wondered at how God interacted with us. I was perhaps at a good starting point as I was already quite a transparent person, but I had to learn to recognize what I needed in those moments and dare to be honest with others and with myself. I often reminded myself that something I shared or said might help someone else. And through all this I had to learn to love myself.'

Like Tola, you may feel that you don't 'deserve' God's forgiveness. Or, like me, you may have struggles with questions about why the person who hurt you 'deserves' to be forgiven. But, as Zeke explained to me, none of us 'deserves' to be forgiven, and that is the point: 'There is grace, and this is something that we don't deserve. As individuals, we sometimes think we have to earn forgiveness or that others have to earn ours, but if we look at Jesus he chose to forgive people and ultimately to die for the sin of all humanity. And even on the cross he prayed for forgiveness for the people around him. If you are really struggling, you can ask God to *help* you to forgive. Remember also that people are a product of sin and broken-ness. The reality is that hurt people hurt people, so for a moment take your eyes off yourself and look at what might have caused the person who has hurt you to act in that way. We need to admit we are struggling, and cry out to God: be honest, reach out to others, to someone who will listen to and pray for us!'

Why is forgiveness so important?

You may not have noticed it, but earlier in this chapter I wrote that I began the process of 'forgiving' God for the things I thought he had let happen. But, as you know by now, grace and forgiveness are all God's idea. Humanity took and misused our free will, turning away from God, and God's story is one of drawing us back into a right relationship with him through his Son, Jesus Christ. Though I do not think my mental health condition is a sin per se, I definitely know there are areas in my life and decisions I have made where I have wilfully turned away from God and, for that, I am so grateful for his forgiveness. Nowhere in the Bible does it say become a Christian and life will be easy, but God does promise to be alongside us through it all, and, at this point in my story, I was finally starting to see that.

In the Bible we read that we ought to 'bear with each other and forgive one another if any of you has a grievance against someone. Forgive as the Lord forgave you' (Colossians 3.13, NIV). We are forgiven. Jesus died for all of our sins. Let that sink in. And it's from this place that our own forgiveness for others flows. If we are angry with God or feel shame in connection with him, this creates a barrier between us that Jesus' blood has already brought down. And yet a responsibility is placed on us to keep acknowledging our sins and repenting, which is a fancy word for simply turning back to God. As we read in 2 Chronicles 7.14 (NIV): 'If my people, who are called by my name, will humble themselves and pray and seek my face and turn from their wicked ways, then I will hear from heaven and I will forgive their sin . . .' And again in 1 John 1:9 (NIV): 'If we confess our sins, he is faithful and just and will forgive us our sins and purify us from all unrighteousness.' Looking back, I can see that I blamed God for so much of my hurt. I viewed God as this angry being who loved everyone else more than me, and this needed to change. I was desperate to feel close to God and to sense his love, but I knew there were barriers there. It was through my honest prayer and getting angry with God that he extended his love to me and encouraged me to ultimately receive his forgiveness and forgive myself.

Then we are told to forgive others. I never thought I could forgive my abuser or others who had hurt me along the way, but I have. One of the reasons I struggled with forgiving my abuser was the fact that I felt that if I did forgive him for what he had done, it was like accepting that what had happened to me was OK. It was far from OK. And yet Jesus doesn't ask us to become best friends with those who have abused us or continue to see them day by day, but he asks us to let go and trust that one day God will put all things right. Romans 3.23–24 (NIV) tells us that 'all have sinned and fall short of the glory of God, and all are justified freely by his grace through the redemption that came by Christ Jesus'. It also assures us in Matthew 25.31–46 that Jesus will judge the world and there will be the justice that so many of us crave in this lifetime. It is God's job to judge and our role to trust. As Hannah Williams said when we sat down together: 'What I find helps when it comes to forgiveness is, firstly, remembering it isn't necessarily about accepting that what has happened is OK or being in a relationship with the person who has hurt you, but about letting go of the hurt caused. It is a daily choice we make, and sometimes we have to keep telling ourselves this is the decision we will make. If we don't forgive it will cause us so much resentment and have a negative impact on our lives.'

Hannah's words rang so true for me. It was only when I chose to forgive and chose *daily* to forgive that I slowly began to feel freer and freer from the control the failure to forgive had had over me. The disciples too must have struggled with forgiveness, as in Matthew 18.21 (NIV) we read: 'Then Peter came to Jesus and asked, "Lord, how many times shall I forgive my brother who sins against me? Up to seven times?" Jesus answered, "I tell you, not seven times, but seventy-seven times."' For Jesus, forgiveness wasn't about keeping score but about losing count.

As I sat at the Alpha Weekend, wrestling with my lack of forgiveness for myself and others, a woman called Pippa shared her story, detailing her own mental illness and how she had lived with it for so long, but God had healed her. And she read these words from Isaiah 61.3 (NIV): 'And provide for those who grieve in Zion – to bestow on them a crown of beauty instead of ashes, the oil of joy instead of mourning, and a garment of praise instead of a spirit of despair. They will be called oaks of righteousness, a planting of the LORD for the display of his splendour.' As I heard those words and spoke to Pippa about them afterwards, I decided to become a Christian. This didn't mean I instantly forgave myself and others, but it set me on a journey. And, I have to say, the more I have chosen daily to receive God's forgiveness and extend it to others, the more I have moved forward in my recovery. It has helped me to heal and let go and stop ruminating over things constantly in my head. Forgiveness can be painful and slow but when we keep being forgiven and forgiving others, there is more freedom to be found.

Practical steps

Step 1: Make a daily choice to surrender and keep saying yes!

Choice is always an interesting topic when it comes to mental health, but I wanted to emphasize that sometimes when we are in recovery from our past and moving on, we need to make a choice each day, and forgiveness can be one of these choices. Jemima Haley at Alpha explained these choices by saying: 'We say a big "yes" to moving forward, but each day we need to say lots more "yeses" and make those choices to step forward.' And in my case this is exactly what my relationship with Jesus, my recovery and my healing from shame have involved. I said a 'yes' at the start of the process but there are moments when I have to consciously choose to not self-sabotage and keep saying 'yes' to yet more life and freedom.

Step 2: Think about those people in your life whom you need to forgive

Make a list of them, perhaps adding details about how they have hurt you. Pray over it, asking God to help you, and then think about how you can bless that person instead; sometimes physical acts such as praying for them or sending a letter can help.

Step 3: Practise gratitude and looking up!

I do think that sometimes when we get trapped in bitterness and unforgivingness we spend so much time going round and round in circles, causing us to focus inwards. We are forgiven by God who sent his only Son to die for us, and so at the very least we can be thankful for that. It's good to try to identify the blessings in life, and this will help us forgive from a place of gratitude.

Prayer

Dear Lord, I am sorry that I find it so hard at times to forgive. Thank you that you love me no matter what; thank you that you are by my side, guiding me through this tricky topic. Thank you for sending your Son to die on the cross. Please help me learn to forgive as you forgive us and to bless those who have hurt me. Amen.

7

Free from it *all*?

'Why is there suffering in the world?' is one of life's biggest questions. If there is an all-loving, all-powerful God, why are so many prayers seemingly left unanswered? Why do so many go through life without being healed? Or why are so many yet to recover from mental illness?

When we think of physical illness there seems to be a clear-cut definition of when healing has occurred or what recovery looks like. You break a leg and you know that when the bone repairs it has healed; you have a headache and recovery comes when the pain goes. And yet when we are looking at our mental health it is sometimes harder to see progress being made or to know whether full healing is possible or when it has occurred. For me, when I think about what recovery from an eating disorder looks like, there is so much that comes to mind – from being physically well, to not having food rules, to recognizing my triggers and actively refusing to turn to unhealthy behaviours in these triggering situations. As the charity Rethink Mental Illness puts it: 'People often talk about clinical and personal recovery. Personal recovery is about working towards something that is important to you.'[19] Importantly, they also remind us of this simple truth: 'You can recover from mental illness.'

That said, when it comes to certain mental illnesses the statistics for full recovery differ; for example, only 50 per cent of people with an eating disorder are reported ever to fully recover. And yet, as I am learning again and again, statistics are no match for the God who can heal and restore all things. I believe this truth so ardently that I am currently campaigning for a society that can visualize full recovery from eating disorders and has the systems in place to see this vision become a reality. I do believe that full recovery is possible. Nevertheless, I would be lying to you if I didn't say that I have times of frustration, disappointment, confusion and doubt that I'll ever fully recover from my mental illness.

As we look to the Bible, we can know that God didn't promise a world free from suffering in this life, but he did promise to be with us as we look ahead to a day when there will be no more tears or suffering, a day in which he will make 'everything new' (Revelation 21.5, NIV). Before we dive further into the topic of hope and healing, I invite you to tell God exactly where you are right now: hopeful? Tired? Worn out? All of these? Remember, God can handle our mess and never asks us to shoulder the burden of our health, healing or recovery alone.

Aren't I meant to be 'new' by now?

A year had passed since I became a Christian and, although I could feel how much better my life was with Jesus at the centre of it, I still felt myself carrying a familiar weight of disappointment – only this time I was more aware of it thanks to becoming more and more acquainted with Jesus' promise of freedom. I was still grappling with so many questions about healing. Since the day after the Alpha Weekend Away I had taken positive steps forward – often blasting worship music around my flat, filled with hope for the future – and then felt myself taking steps 'back', getting stuck in the same cycles that had plagued my life before I gave it back to God: feeling unloved by God, as if something was wrong with me and therefore I was not worthy of being healed. It felt as if recovery was a roller-coaster ride.

Then the pandemic hit. As 2020 began, stories came in from around the world of this new virus, one that no one had heard of before, which was shaking the world and instilling fear across our nation. The news stories started off quite sporadic but by the middle of March most of the world had been thrust into national lockdowns. And as the fear began to get an ever-greater grip, in the UK society's way of coping was to go to the supermarket and stockpile, which seemed like a harmless coping mechanism at the time, but was perhaps one that had a lot attached to it. As I sat watching on, as my work and resultant income were getting cancelled, as even our time outside became limited, I was feeling more and more out of control. I kept clinging to God, trying to pray, trying to listen, but even that was hard at times. I tried running and praying, praying for those who had hurt me; I even tried 'outsourcing' my prayers – paying an elderly couple who offered a prayer service (something I would not necessarily recommend!), but time and time again God was reminding me that sometimes we just have to sit in the painful place and do the hard work of choosing to trust in him, again and again, day in, day out, for our ultimate recovery.

Throughout the pandemic, many of us became more aware of our health – both physical and mental – than ever before. All around us, people were getting ill, some dying and some recovering, with the world both questioning what was happening and also rediscovering togetherness (remember, in the UK, clapping the workers of the NHS from our doorsteps?), and in many cases turning to prayer, with a recent report showing that young people in the UK are twice as likely as older people to pray regularly.[20] In such a time of suffering and unanswered questions, I know that confusion and the desire for control can run rife. And yet, on the days when I was able to be honest with God and let my confusion become curiosity, I began to see him at work in the small, faithful steps on my road to recovery. I pray that, as you look at the following contrasting stories I am about to share, you will know that wherever you are on the spectrum of mental health, no matter where you are in your recovery, you are not alone.

All at once and one step at a time

The famous quote 'Comparison is the thief of joy' – often attributed to President Theodore Roosevelt – rings true for many of us when it comes to our journey of recovery from poor mental health. And yet the Bible often encourages us to share stories of what God has done, to encourage one another. In the writing of this book, I spoke to two incredible women with two hugely contrasting stories of God's work in their lives. As you read these accounts, I encourage you not to compare your own journey with those of these women but instead to look to God and how he is always at work, even if we struggle to see it at times.

Pippa's story

'I grew up in a loving family and have many happy memories of my childhood. However, things changed when I hit my teenage years as I began to have major insecurities about the way I looked and struggled with my body image. I ended up being rebellious and attention-seeking, possibly in an attempt to control or overcome the uncomfortable and hurtful experiences of my life, and unfortunately I ended up with bulimia. This eating disorder went on for 12 years, through my later teens and most of my 20s.'

'To be honest, for most of the time I was ill I didn't perceive it to be a big problem, although I felt a lot of shame about it, and so I didn't ever speak of it with anyone, even my family. Once I embarked upon my career, though, the eating disorder became something that didn't sit comfortably with my role as an officer in the Royal

Air Force. I felt in some way that the integrity of my leadership was being compromised by bulimia, so I pursued a way out.'

'I tried counselling, hypnotherapy, Reiki and simply trying really hard to give it up, but it had become such a strong addiction that none of these things gave me freedom. Then in my late 20s I had a completely unexpected encounter with God that changed the trajectory of my life and which, within a short time, gave me total healing and freedom from bulimia. I still can't believe the transformation – from years of acute illness and addiction to a life of completely normal eating in a matter of weeks, void of relapse and any temptation to make myself ill. Jesus totally broke the power of addiction in my life and started me on the path of self-acceptance and a life of authenticity and freedom. I look back on it now and perceive that the miraculous had occurred; I had become so bound up in bulimia – sometimes being ill five times a day – but after only a few sessions of prayer ministry I was completely set free. There was no gradual change over time for me – it was pure instant freedom that I experienced.'

Liz's story

'I didn't grow up a Christian and I spent most of my teenage years with clinical depression. I was on medication and had a lot of therapy. I now struggle less with depression but have anxiety that has not been healed. Historically this has not been addressed very well in church, and often people would say, "Pray about it and it will get better." This used to be really frustrating to hear but I had a few realizations during my own journey. Firstly, God does not inflict them, but he can use the thorns in our sides. Anxiety is my thorn, and it has opened doors for me. It has also helped bring about a degree of humility – without my anxiety, perhaps I would not be able to relate to people quite as much. I share my story and my experience and talk freely about it and it has helped me realize the hidden battles so many people face. As Christians, we should be shoulder to shoulder in living vulnerably and, in that vulnerability, we can find healing. As for my own story, I managed to find a way of accepting my circumstances and stopped feeling angry, as I sensed God was using them. I remember hearing preachers Rick and Kay Warren explain that, throughout life, we all experience mountain-tops and valleys. There are some people in life and in the Church who are operating out of the valleys even though they don't know whether or when the mountaintop will ever come. These people show true strength. We need to move away from calling these people vulnerable, because actually they are brave! They are brave for turning up today, tomorrow and the next day. And the reality is, it isn't over until it is over. As Christians, we always know we are a work in progress. Tomorrow we will be a little more like Jesus. This is the hope that I hold on to, knowing that the Holy Spirit is with me and can mentor me to that point.'

As you can see, both Pippa and Liz experienced God's healing power, but in two completely different ways. I was really inspired by Pippa's story the first time she shared it with me, but I also found Liz's account of day-to-day, slow, inner healing refreshing. God experienced pain and is with us in our own pain. He also has plans and dreams for our healing that are more than we could 'ask or imagine' (Ephesians 3.20, NIV). Even in Pippa's case, where she experienced instant freedom from her eating disorder, she shared with me how God had much more far-reaching plans of deliverance for her than she could ever have thought of herself.

'Freedom from the grips of bulimia was only the beginning, as God began to deal with the roots of the problem,' Pippa told me. 'I found the issue was not bulimia itself but a whole raft of other things that needed to be addressed: self-rejection, the pain of rejection, anger and rebellion, feeling controlled, and many other issues... While I think that self-help programmes and professional support can be helpful on the road to recovery, I believe the key to lasting and absolute freedom lies in Jesus. The unique gospel message is that Jesus overcame the power of sin and evil, absorbing it into himself on the cross, and by doing so he gave his followers access to the same victory and power. Put simply, if we receive him as Lord in our lives, we have access to all of God's promises, including freedom and peace. Once we have accepted Christ, there is a journey that our heavenly Father wants to take us on to be able to discover the power and truth of the gospel message. This starts with understanding our identity as his beloved children. Jesus modelled this 'sonship' for us in a radical way – he knew the Father as his dad and even called him 'Daddy'! This familiarity with God was considered heretical at the time and it was this kind of talk that actually got him killed. Yet it was this Father–Son relationship that enabled Jesus to undertake his radical and miraculous ministry. This intimacy also enabled him to live immune to worldly performance pressures. He was no man's puppet or pawn, being thoroughly secure in himself. Through Jesus, we can know exactly the same love and affirmation from the Father; each of us can profoundly encounter the Father's love as we approach him. As we experience this love for ourselves and internalize the loving truth expressed in Bible passages, our minds become renewed and our lives are transformed. The result is that we can live a countercultural life as Jesus did, free of performance pressure and enslavement to other people's opinions or demands. I experienced all this for myself, and over time I began to see myself the way the Father sees me – as his precious, beloved daughter – and other people's opinions of me became unimportant. In God I discovered that I can truly be me – I have nothing to prove to anyone, as God's love and affirmation are more precious and profound than anything else. I have also come to accept and love myself because I live daily with a tangible sense of God's unconditional love and affirmation simply for being his daughter; it's the same love that I have for my children – there's nothing they could do to stop me from loving them. I found that issues to do with self-rejection, anger and painful experiences could all be dealt with through this unconditional love. I have realized that it is only his voice that counts for all eternity, and this heart knowledge has given me confidence, purpose and lasting freedom.'

'There is nothing that he can't redeem if we are prepared to share it with him,' Pippa went on. 'His way involves allowing him to become the most important thing in our life. His path leads us out of brokenness and is truly transformational, but we have to choose his way for ourselves; it's a choice that many of us find difficult, as it requires humility and daily surrender of our life to him – something that can be foreign to many of us, as we have been conditioned to be self-sufficient rather than truly dependent on God.'

'I understand that some people may struggle with my story of such a dramatic healing from bulimia, just as I have struggled in other areas of my life where God hasn't brought about the instant change I have sought. But I have come to realize that God always wants to rescue us "through" the problem, not just "from" it, so that we might have lasting freedom. So, although I was healed of the addiction to bulimia, I still needed to journey with God to weed out the underlying problems; otherwise I could have relapsed, or the root issues might have manifested themselves in other ways. We have to trust God's direction and journey for healing, whether it is immediate or a longer process. We can become fixated on the healing alone, but I have realized that there's a much more significant and lasting transformation that God wants for us, and that is the healing of our soul . . .'

A new creation

'Therefore, if anyone is in Christ, the new creation has come: the old has gone, the new is here!' the apostle Paul says in 2 Corinthians 5.17

(NIV). And yet, when I became a Christian, I felt that I had taken a lot of the 'old stuff' with me. I confess that, whenever I think of what it means to be healed in the Bible, my mind automatically goes to the stories of Jesus' miracles of physical and instant healing as recorded in the Gospels. One of my favourite stories is in Luke 17.11–19, where Jesus heals the lepers; among many things, this story shows us that Jesus goes to those in society who are outcast or broken and he doesn't lose sight of them. I love reading these accounts, but what I failed to notice initially is that Jesus is healing people physically, but is also cleansing them of their sins and healing them spiritually. In other places in the Bible, Jesus doesn't heal immediately, for example in John 11.1–44 (NIV), where he finds out his friend Lazarus is ill but 'delays' visiting him for two days, during which Lazarus dies. In this case Jesus has so much confidence that death isn't the end that he tells his followers: 'This sickness will not end in death. No, it is for God's glory so that God's Son may be glorified through it,' before later raising Lazarus from the dead. We too can be confident that, no matter what our circumstances are, God is with us in our suffering and is in control even when we don't understand or see it. As theologian Claire Williams shared with me: 'There is a type of "theodicy" that tries to solve the problem of evil. But we do know that God does not cause this suffering, so while it is OK to be frustrated and angry with God, and indeed we sit within a long tradition of lament in the Bible that practises this, if you haven't yet been healed or if you are suffering right now, it is important to hold on to this truth: the Bible says God is good; he is powerful. The world is chaotic, but God is in control; God knows and God sees. We don't suffer on our own. We have God's gaze on us.'

In the Bible, we are told to 'ask' God for what we need (Matthew 7.7, NIV) and to 'pray without ceasing' (1 Thessalonians 5.16, ESV), not because God is withholding things from us but because he wants us to be in communion with him. In Luke 18 we read the story of the persistent woman: a reminder to keep praying, to keep going, to keep communicating through hard times. We can be honest with God throughout; we will never sound like a broken record to him. As Ruth Kirkland, the youth worker in Hertfordshire, shared with me: 'When I pray for someone and they aren't healed, it can be really disappointing. I have to take that disappointment back to Jesus and ask him for forgiveness for believing lies like: God doesn't hear me; God won't answer my prayers; God doesn't care. I remind myself of his nature and trust in his character: in his goodness, kindness, faithfulness and love. I do this through reading the Bible and spending time with God in prayer and through worship. I remind myself that there is a bigger picture that I cannot see and that I need to leave the outcome to God, and I try to continue to pray for others. I have heard that comparison is the thief of joy and I know this to be true. It can be so easy to compare, and one of the ways I help myself is by not allowing my mind to go there at all; if an unhelpful thought comes into my head, I stop it right there and don't allow myself to entertain it. If it is comparison with another Christian, I remind myself that we are all on the same team and the most important thing is bringing glory to God and telling others about Jesus, and that it is not really about me at all. As I grow more secure in God's love for me and his view of me, I find myself caring less about what others are like or what they are doing, and I grow in gratitude for my own gifts and for how God has made me instead. Praying for others, cheering others on and blessing them are also great ways to put myself second and take the focus off myself too.'

Pete Greig emphasizes the importance of petitionary prayer in his book *How to Pray*,[21] explaining that God wants us to ask for things, not only because it is showing a vulnerable side to us but because asking for things is normal when we are in a relationship with someone. We have that direct access to God and so we can use it. He might not answer our prayers exactly as we had hoped, but he is always wanting to bless us. As Matt Hogg, vicar of St Alban's Fulham, shared with me: 'It is important to remember that healing looks different for everyone. For some it is an ongoing process, and while there may be a certain moment that Christians call salvation, where you choose to put your faith and trust in God, the process itself is still very real. In Galatians 5 we are reminded of the love, joy and peace we can find in Jesus; even in the midst of pain, God is there.'

Practical steps

Step 1: Identify the mountain that God can help you climb

Sometimes when my thoughts become overwhelming, I find that drawing a mountain and writing all the things on my mind inside it can help capture the thoughts. Then I draw myself on top of the mountain (a stick figure is just fine) and write words of Scripture around myself. The Bible promises that 'if [we] have faith as small as a mustard seed, [we] can say to this mountain "Move from here to there" and it will move. Nothing will be impossible for [us]' (Matthew 17.20, NIV), so begin telling yourself that God can move any mountain you face.

Step 2: Stop comparing your journey with those of others and start looking for where God is at work

As we have already seen, God's healing looks different for everybody. Fix your eyes on God and ask him to highlight where he is already working in your life and to give you a vision for the freedom he is asking you to step into next.

Step 3: Be persistent and honest in prayer

Liz admitted to praying the same prayers over and over again. This isn't insanity; this is what God asks us to do. She shared how, when her anxiety is really bad, she prays the same written prayer repeatedly, knowing that the repetition will help reframe her thoughts until one day the prayer will eventually 'pray' her.

Prayer

Dear God, I know that at times I have found it hard to deal with the disappointment of not being healed or of not being further along in my recovery, but please help me to trust you in the process. Please guide me in these moments and put people in my life who will help me to deal with what life is often throwing at me and consistently point me to you. Amen.

8

Free to hope

'Do you really want to find freedom?' I don't know about you, but at first glance this seems like a stupid question. Of *course* I want to feel free. And yet there have been times in my journey when I have wondered what it would be like for me to be healed from my mental health problem for good: who would I be without it? What would my excuse be if I didn't feel like doing something? What if I couldn't point to things from my past to explain why I am the way I am? What if I just don't have the strength to hope any more?

Now I can see that, at points in my life, my mental illness has become part of my identity; I have sometimes found it easier to be the 'victim' rather than do the hard work of recovery. Victimhood isn't a new phenomenon, but something that has been around for decades. Rahav Gabay, Doctor of Psychology at Tel Aviv University, defines this tendency for interpersonal victimhood as 'an ongoing feeling that the self is a victim, which is generalized across many kinds of relationships. As a result, victimization becomes a central part of the individual's identity'.[22] She goes on to explain that the resulting behaviours can include rumination over past events, constantly seeking recognition for the victimhood, and struggling to forgive people. If we're not careful, some of us can fall into a sort of Victimhood Olympics, competing over who has it worst, as in the scene in Roger Michell's classic 1999 rom-com *Notting Hill* where characters at a dinner party put forward a case for the most deserving 'victim' to decide who gets the last brownie.

Please don't think I'm suggesting that having poor mental health or a mental health condition is a choice. I know I would never *choose* to suffer from an eating disorder. And yet I know there are choices to be made when it comes to pursuing hope. Have you ever felt that you have a friend who enjoys looking after you when you feel upset but seems to distance themselves when you are happy? We need to make sure we are surrounding ourselves with people who help us make healthy mental and physical choices to shrug off victimhood, to be set free from lack of forgiveness and to pursue God's plans and purpose for our redemption.

Reaching a plateau

It was the summer of 2020, and I was ambling around the baking-hot city of Milan with my friend Lauren during the 'travel window' between the UK's national lockdowns. Having found the isolation caused by not being able to worship in person with my church community during the pandemic particularly hard, I was glad to have the opportunity to put the 'world to rights' with a solidly faith-filled friend. We talked about love, happiness, God and everything in between, and that's when Lauren asked me what stage I was at in my recovery from my illness. As she did this, she told me about a talk she had heard by preacher and author Christine Caine, entitled 'Get Off the Mat'.[23] In this talk Christine noted that there are elements of choice that we make in our healing process, and that although God is 100 per cent in control, there are things that we can do ourselves to help us move into a space of victory.

As I got into bed that evening – hugging an ice pack as we'd somehow failed to book an Airbnb® with air conditioning – I thought about Lauren's question. I had been out of hospital for over a decade and survived one relapse, but at the same time I realized that I had probably become settled in my recovery; I was healthy but ate a lot of the same foods, did the same sort of exercise and was quite regimented in various areas of my life. I felt the distinct stirring of the idea that, although I had gained more freedom than I had had in the past, God offered me even more. It was there that I committed myself to challenging my recovery every day, from having foods that I might find scary to eat to intentionally ordering the things from the menu that I actually wanted, not just what were the lowest in calories or 'healthiest' for me. I asked God to help me to be louder than the voice in my head that told me I 'can't' or 'mustn't' or 'shouldn't'. It was uncomfortable at first, but this time I knew I was committed to playing the 'long game' with God by my side. I was hopeful of healing but in the meantime knew I needed to slow down, to stop rushing, and to put one foot deliberately in front of the other and keep moving *with* hope and towards God.

Stepping into victory

A well-timed question from a good friend set a string of thoughts in motion for me, and the biggest realization it prompted was that if I'm not moving forward in my recovery, I have in fact stopped moving altogether, reaching a plateau when it comes to progress. There is so much in the Bible about moving *towards* Jesus, becoming *more* of who we are intended to become, *running* the race marked out for us (Hebrews 12), and we can make a decision to keep moving with God. As primary school adviser for the London Diocesan Board for Schools Mary Thorne explained: 'The first thing is the desire to move forward in our recovery with God; is it a real want or not? The journey really starts only when we have the desire to change. As a person of faith, it means I have had to accept that I am not in control. This is really hard; if we expose ourselves to mystery then we need to respond to what comes our way. If you have a desire to change, who can accompany you? And once you have that person or people, recognize that we all go backwards and forwards all the time and that is all right!'

Though God is in control, Mary's words highlight yet again that we have a part to play: 'How do you prepare to welcome God? If we welcome a guest into our home we prepare a lot, but are we doing this with God? We often find excuses not to sit and be present. Even when I am in church, I sometimes busy myself with ministry so that I am focusing on others. I am aware that in reality some of these patterns can become a bit of an avoidance tactic.'

In many ways, it is strange that we can so long to sit with God and yet so often find distractions and excuses that mean we end up seeking peace in all things *but* God. Sometimes we get so 'comfy' with what we know that we don't trust that God has better things for us. We can't ignore the fact that such 'distractions' can be a tactic of the enemy, as can the lie that God will only approach us with judgement. Well-being coach Jon Toms drilled home the importance of remembering God's character in our desire to spend time with him: 'If we just see God as a God of judgement, it means we feel God is always frowning on us and looking down on us. But if we see God as a God of love and someone who wants to be inti-mate with us, then that God of love will help us to love ourselves. It is a continuous journey; there are ups and downs, but our relation-ship with God should enable us to come to him with everything.'

This ability to come to God with anything was really evident as Revd Matt Hogg shared his story with me, as was our human tendency to seek peace in so many places other than God: 'I grew up in a Christian home and my dad was a vicar,' Matt began. 'Because of this, I had certain pressures put on me – not intentionally, but it just happened. When I left home and came to London, I could do what *I* wanted to do. For me, real freedom looked like drinking, doing drugs and going out all the time. But it was never enough for me, and I remember a time when I ended up in hospital after an overdose, just lying there thinking "How can this be the picture of freedom? This is so far from life in all its fullness." Shortly after that, I went on a lads' holiday, returned home and was sitting in my bedroom at my parents' house with a hacking smoker's cough, and my brother knocked on the door. He wanted to pray for me. When he left the room, tears welled up in my eyes. They weren't bad tears but good ones, tears of recognition that God was right there.' This sparked Matt to develop a faith of his own and even to go on to become a vicar himself, but this doesn't mean his journey of finding 'freedom' is complete. 'For me, the process is continuous and I am becoming more and more free to love God more and more,' Matt shared with me honestly. 'I am still tempted to look for freedom in other things. It's no longer drugs or alcohol, but it might be something more subtle, like relying on caffeine or gaining my self-worth from social media, or work. These temporary fixes are short-term solutions rather than the permanent freedom that comes from fullness of life in Jesus. In the moment it may feel as if we are making a bit of progress, but we need to have faith that God is working on things already. God may be calling us to step out. The truth is that God is at work and we have a choice about whether to join in, and sometimes we choose not to, but he is patient with us. He tells us to "come" and trust him, and I believe that in the painful moments of life he speaks really tenderly to us.'

Once again, we can see that there is a holy dynamic between *knowing* that God is in control and is already working and *choosing* to be active in joining in with what God is doing. So how can we create an environment in which we are choosing to partner with God daily? 'Spiritual disciplines are the key,' Matt explained clearly. 'I stay fit physically by walking and moving, and in the same way

I have an opportunity to become spiritually fit, and this comes from reading and living out the truths in the Bible. A number of years ago, I actually laminated a bunch of "I am" statements from the Scriptures and stuck them on my shower wall so that I am reminded of who God says I am each day as I wash. For me, it is my identity that can sometimes feel under attack. The enemy tries to sow doubts in our minds, so I need to remind myself that my identity is found in Christ. I am a child of God, called by him, and this is always my starting point. I make sure that I am reminding myself practically of what God says about me and then spend time praying and meditating on Scripture. I love the idea that God is encamped around us, protecting us. And, finally, it is so important to be accountable to a community – you don't need to tell everyone everything, but being honest with certain people is really helpful.'

My talk with Zeke Rink from Dreaming the Impossible reinforced this truth, that we were not designed to walk out our faith alone: 'Jesus says that in this world we will have troubles, but there is a way through the pains of life, and so much of it is about recognizing that with some challenges we need to be prepared to go on a long, painful journey through them and find a community to do it with. This takes bravery, honesty and self-reflection.' I know that, for me personally, being accountable to friends like Lauren, who are willing to ask uncomfortable questions and get to the core of how I am really doing, is central in my pursuing hope and freedom with God.

More than conquerors

In John 16.33 (NIV), it says: 'I have told you these things, so that in me you may have peace. In this world you will have trouble. But take heart! I have overcome the world.' Let that sink in: Jesus has overcome the world. And yet too often we feel defeated by the ongoing battle in this lifetime. But God doesn't leave us to work this out alone; he has sent us the Holy Spirit to work within us and through us, and Christ continues to fight for our freedom. As we read in Romans 8 (NIV):

> What, then, shall we say in response to these things? If God is for us, who can be against us? He who did not spare his own Son, but gave him up for us all – how will he not also, along with him, graciously give us all things? Who will bring any charge against those whom God has chosen? It is God who justifies. Who then is the one who condemns? No one. Christ Jesus who died – more than that, who was raised to life – is at the right hand of God and is also interceding for us. Who shall separate us from the love of Christ? Shall trouble or hardship or persecution or famine or nakedness or danger or sword? As it is written: 'For your sake we face death all day long; we are considered as sheep to be slaughtered.' No, in all these things we are more than conquerors through him who loved us.

We aren't going to have a trouble-free life as Christians, but we know that, because we have God in our lives, we can overcome whatever is thrown at us! How amazing is that? Even though life is hard, God is right here with us. We can remind the enemy every single day that the battle has already been won – we are a new creation in Jesus and have his resurrection power. This yields more and more strength for all of us. And, remember, we don't have to be perfect; we just have to be persistent. As Zeke told me: 'When you go down a dead end, you cannot fast-track getting out of it. It is like when you get to a cul-de-sac: you can't get out, so you have to go back and find another way. Part of our journey with recovery is recognizing where we went wrong. Recognizing what has affected us, not going along with this, and forgiving others if they have said stuff over us. Forgiveness, sharing and communication have been the keys for me to step forward. We were not made to be alone. We need deep conversations in a trusting and non-judgemental way. The church is meant to provide that, but we need to remember that the church is made up of a community of broken people. I do struggle to believe the narrative that people will never get better – it might be a battle, it might be a challenge and it might be part of your thinking, but it does not need to control you.'

We are born to be in community, and as people who follow Jesus we are conquerors, we are an army, working together against a common enemy. As we read in Ephesians 6.10–18 (NIV):

> Finally, be strong in the Lord and his mighty power. Put on the full armour of God, so that you can take your stand against the devil's schemes. For our struggle is not against flesh and blood, but against the rulers, against the authorities, against the powers of this dark world and against the spiritual forces of evil in the heavenly realms. Therefore, put on the full armour of God, so that when the day of evil comes, you may be able to stand your ground, and after you have done everything, to stand. Stand firm then, with the belt of truth buckled around your waist, with the breastplate of righteousness in place, and with your feet fitted with the readiness that comes from the gospel of peace. In addition to all this, take up the shield of faith, with which you can extinguish all the flaming arrows of the evil one. Take the helmet of salvation and the sword of the Spirit, which is the word of God. And pray in the Spirit on all occasions with all kinds of prayers and requests. With this in mind, be alert and always keep on praying for all the Lord's people.

Here we read that putting on the armour of God includes knowing the truth, living out the gospel of peace, exercising faith, reading the word of God: essentially practising the spiritual disciplines that Matt Hogg mentions have been so essential to his discipleship. The spiritual disciplines are the exercises that lead to the fruit of the Spirit that we read about in Galatians 5.22–23 (NIV), namely: 'love, joy, peace, forbearance, kindness, goodness, faithfulness, gentleness and self-control'. Author and preacher John Mark Comer highlights in his book *Live No Lies* that 'there's no official list of practices of Jesus. Technically, any habit you see in the life or teachings of Jesus is a spiritual discipline. But there are two anchor practices for our fight with the devil that Jesus put on display in the desert.'[24] John Mark names these as 'quiet prayer' and 'Scripture'.

If you've been a Christian for some time or even if you've just got this far in this book, you'll know that prayer and reading the Bible are central to the Christian life, but so many of us can struggle with making time for them. I think God knew we might find it hard to prioritize such practices amid the busyness of life, as he tells us to 'be still, and know that I am God' (Psalm 46.10, NIV). I know that I find being still really hard. My brain goes all over the place, I get frustrated when I don't hear from God straight away, and so I find it easier to keep myself busy with my usual patterns and activities. And yet, when I make time to simply rest and be with God – even if just for a few minutes a day – I do find that the peace I am searching for is deposited in my heart. Not every day, not always, but as I turn up daily I find my heart and mind slowing and myself knowing more and more that God is who he says he is and will deliver all that he has promised to us, his children. And, as I create this space to feel his love and experience his grace, I find myself extending them to others. Instead of flying off the handle and playing the victim, I find myself taking time to recognize what is triggering me and responding with more kindness and understanding. Living with a mental health condition is hard, but there are choices at our disposal that can make it easier. Choosing to be still enough to centre ourselves, to know how we are feeling, to share this with others and, above all, to know that God is God, are all choices on offer to us here, today.

Practical steps

Step 1: Research the 'victim mentality' and ask if you can see any of this in yourself

This step will not apply to everyone. There are plenty of people living with poor mental health or mental illness who do not slip into victimhood at all. But for those of us who can recognize that we've let our mental state become a large part of our identity and perhaps cause us to slip into this victim mindset, it might be helpful to stop and ask God to help us identify any self-destructive thought patterns at play.

Step 2: Identify things that might be stopping you from hoping

Following my trip to Milan and my friend's challenge to me, I got pretty ruthless with the things I was allowing to keep me stuck in my recovery. I stopped listening to podcasts that were not helpful for me and 'unfollowed' a lot of accounts that fuelled my tendency to compare and fed my anxiety. Are there things that you need to let go of today in order to hold on to hope?

Step 3: Be still and be kind to yourself

Try being 'still' for five minutes a day, whether in silence or with worship music on in the background. Ask God to help you settle your thoughts. Perhaps try reading a psalm a day. But be kind to yourself if you miss a day or have a day when you lose hope. There is always tomorrow, and God's grace is big enough to cover all your confusion and cul-de-sacs.

Prayer

Dear Lord, I so long to move into a space where life feels victorious. Please help me to identify the things that hinder me from knowing the hope of the gospel, and to find the strength to step forwards with your support, your love and your guidance. Amen.

Love has the final word

'Love is patient, love is kind . . .' These words probably sound familiar to you, whether you've been a Christian for a long time or are exploring faith for the first time. These words are spoken at weddings all over the world – I even had them at my own wedding, which took place as I was in the process of writing this book. Though they can often seem overused, if we take the time to read them, sit with them and really *know* them, I believe they can change our lives for ever – no matter where we find ourselves on the mental health spectrum at the present time.

As we have seen, there are many different causes of poor mental health and mental illness – some biological, some circumstantial, some we might not understand this side of heaven. And yet I believe that if we truly know the love of God and are able to extend this love to ourselves and others, it will be a massive game changer when it comes to our journey with mental health, not just when we are 'healed' or 'feel better' but right here, right now, precisely where we find ourselves at this very moment.

In my case, I think a lot of my mental illness is rooted in the fact that I never felt loved. This doesn't mean I didn't grow up in a loving household but simply that I always struggled to believe it, spending many days, weeks and months feeling 'not good enough' and then believing the lie that the reason I wasn't healed from my eating disorder was that God didn't truly love me enough. This led me to feel that I needed to earn love from others. But the thing is, God's love isn't a 'feeling' and we don't need to 'feel' it to *know* it.

In 1 Corinthians 13.4–7 (NIV) we read:

> Love is patient, love is kind. It does not envy, it does not boast, it is not proud. It does not dishonour others, it is not self-seeking, it is not easily angered, it keeps no record of wrongs. Love does not delight in evil but rejoices with the truth. It always protects, always trusts, always hopes, always perseveres.

I once heard someone describe the entire Bible as God's love letter to us, and it certainly is that through and through. From the story of Adam and Eve, where God made humans in his image with no shame, to Jesus' dying on the cross for us, extending his everlasting, unconditional love that we don't have to earn, every page sings of his love for us.

This love is nothing like the version we are shown by Hollywood or see plastered across the squares of social media. So much of the love we see today is a love with conditions, one that loves only if you love in return, one that not everyone can find, and if you have it, you're at risk of losing it. In contrast, God's love is for everyone – no matter how broken or bruised we may be. And God's love is for now – not for when we get ourselves 'fixed' or 'cleaned up'. It is God's love that does the cleaning.

In C. S. Lewis's 1960 book *The Four Loves*, the author describes four types of love: storge (empathy), philia (friendship), eros (romantic love) and agape (unconditional love). It is the agape love that God extends to us through sending his Son, Jesus, to die on the cross. We don't need to strive for anything from God; he has a plan for our lives and loves us even when things feel hard. In the Bible we are reminded about God being constantly for us, reassured that everything God does is influenced by his love for us. Any time we feel as if God is 'punishing' us for not being 'good enough' or for messing up again and again, we can remind ourselves of his unchanging character and his steadfast love. Anna Hodges at HTB Church shared with me that, whenever she is in this situation, she asks herself: 'What is the nature of God right now? There might be pain, but God is loving, and I believe that his goodness and mercy are running after me. I need to keep leaning into God's nature.'

From this place of leaning into God's love, we can then extend it to ourselves and others. In Matthew 22.36–40 (NIV) we read 'the greatest commandment in the Law', which is to 'love the Lord your God with all your heart and with all your soul and with all your mind. This is the first and greatest commandment. And the second is like it: "Love your neighbour as yourself."' I'm not sure about you, but I sometimes find loving myself hard, particularly when I'm experiencing periods of poor mental health. This is something that Tola Doll Fisher, editor and author, has struggled with too: 'In order to get to a place where I could accept God's love I really had to learn from others, but also learn to love myself. I am still learning both these things but, looking back over my life, I can see a shift in my thinking. When I was younger, I was a model and I spent so much of that time not feeling good enough. So I started to surround myself with encouragement from God's Word; not only is this about having Bible verses, but reminding myself that God works all things out. And then practical self-care. I check in with myself: have I drunk enough water? Have I laughed at all today?'

Self-care can sometimes be overlooked in church communities as we seek not to be self-serving, but looking after ourselves doesn't need to be selfish. Though it is not in the Bible, I find this definition of self-love, written in *Psychologies* magazine, helpful: 'Self-love is not simply a state of feeling good. It is a state of appreciation for oneself that *grows from actions* that support our physical, psychological, and spiritual growth.'[25] Self-love is not an obsession with self, and we must be careful that we don't start to idolize it or the practices connected with it, but having a healthy love for ourselves means honouring how God has made us and who he has made us to be. Clothing ourselves in God's love, we can love ourselves – exactly how and where we are – and extend this love to others.

God knows that we need his agape love. I wrote this book during the COVID-19 pandemic, a time which presented a huge range of challenges and left an already devastating epidemic of mental health problems at an all-time high. I know many of us are still looking for answers to why we or our loved ones are still struggling (myself included), but I promise that you are free to love and be loved by an almighty loving Father in the here and now. It is in this position of being loved and loving others that I believe we can all find the endurance to persist in prayer and hold out in hope for full healing from mental illness. This might look different for different people, and some of us might not find that full freedom until the other side of eternity, but that doesn't mean we can't keep hoping for it. Keeping going day after day is not always easy, but even in the midst of the pandemic I know countless people who are able to share stories of hope, stories of joy in slowing down and simplifying life. And even if that wasn't your story, that's all right. For I am sure that 'neither death nor life, neither angels nor demons, neither the present nor the future, nor any powers, neither height nor depth, nor anything else in all creation, will be able to separate us from the love of God that is in Christ Jesus our Lord' (Romans 8.37–39, NIV), and it is for freedom Christ has set us free.

Notes

1 <www.centreformentalhealth.org.uk/publications/covid-19-and-nations-mental-health-may-2021>.

2 <www.mondovo.com/keywords/most-asked-questions-on-google>.

3 <www.psychologytoday.com/gb/blog/how-raise-happy-cooperative-child/202008/middle-child-syndrome>.

4 Name changed for anonymity.

5 <www.mentalhealth.org.uk/publications/body-image-report>.

6 Christine Caine, *Unashamed* (Zondervan, Grand Rapids, MI, 2016).

7 <www.psychologytoday.com/gb/basics/fear>.

8 <www.mentalhealth.org.uk/get-involved/im-fine>.

9 Please note that I went into hospital back in 2007, when children's services were not overstretched like they are today. In fact, when I was in treatment there were empty beds. Please don't compare your story with mine; if you have been turned away from services for not being 'thin enough' or 'not looking as if you have an eating disorder', I am sorry. You do not need to lose more weight to prove anything to anyone; you deserve support no matter what size or shape you are.

10 <www.psychologies.co.uk/understanding-post-traumatic-growth>.

11 </www.healthyplace.com/abuse/abuse-information/what-is-abuse-abuse-definition>.

12 <www.rosscenter.com/news/self-blame/>.

13 <www.psychologytoday.com/us/blog/your-personal-renaissance/201906/why-talking-about-our-problems-makes-us-feel-better>.

14 <https://pubmed.ncbi.nlm.nih.gov/17576282/>.

15 Liz Kelly, Jo Lovett and Linda Regan, *A Gap or a Chasm? Attrition*

in reported rape cases (Home Office Research, Development and Statistics Directorate, London, 2005).

16 <www.bbc.co.uk/news/uk-53588705>.

17 Glennon Doyle, *Untamed* (The Dial Press, New York, 2020).

18 <www.apa.org/monitor/2017/01/ce-corner>.

19 <www.rethink.org/advice-and-information/living-with-mental-illness/treatment-and-support/recovery/>.

20 <www.bbc.co.uk/news/uk-58681075>.

21 Pete Greig, *How to Pray* (Hodder & Stoughton, London, 2019).

22 <www.scientificamerican.com/article/unraveling-the-mindset-of-victimhood/>.

23 <www.youtube.com/watch?v=BSuMzsBFCuQ>.

24 John Mark Comer, *Live No Lies: Recognize and Resist the Three Enemies That Sabotage Your Peace* (Form, London, 2021).

25 <www.psychologytoday.com/us/blog/get-hardy/201203/seven-step-prescription-self-love>.

Resources

If anything from this book has resonated with you, I would really encourage you to reach out for support. Reaching out for support is not weak or something to be embarrassed about; in fact, showing vulnerability is a real strength. I normally find writing it down really helpful: 'I feel X; I have been feeling X for X amount of time; I really need . . .' I also find having a distraction in place after I have reached out for support really helpful too, as it alleviates some of the fear and guilt.

Websites:

Anorexia & Bulimia Care (ABC): <www.anorexiabulimiacare.org.uk>

Crisis Text Line: <www.crisistextline.org>; 24/7 crisis support UK text 85258

F.E.A.S.T.: <www.feast-ed.org>

The Hub of Hope: <https://hubofhope.co.uk>

Kintsugi Hope: <www.kintsugihope.com>

Mind and Soul: <www.mindandsoulfoundation.org>

The Mix: <www.themix.org.uk>

Samaritans: <www.samaritans.org>; 24-hour service call 116 123; email jo@samaritans.org

YoungMinds: <www.youngminds.org.uk>

Courses:

Keys To Freedom: <www.mercyuk.org/keystofreedom> (Christian discipleship)

tastelife: <www.tastelifeuk.org>

WE HAVE A VISION OF A WORLD IN WHICH EVERYONE IS TRANSFORMED BY CHRISTIAN KNOWLEDGE

As well as being an award-winning publisher, SPCK is the oldest Anglican mission agency in the world.

Our mission is to lead the way in creating books and resources that help everyone to make sense of faith.

Will you partner with us to put good books into the hands of prisoners, great assemblies in front of schoolchildren and reach out to people who have not yet been touched by the Christian faith?

To donate, please visit www.spckpublishing.co.uk/donate or call our friendly fundraising team on 020 7592 3900.

An easy way to get to know the Bible

'For those who've been putting aside two years in later life to read the Bible from cover to cover, the good news is: the most important bits are here.' Jeremy Vine, BBC Radio 2

The Bible is full of dramatic stories that have made it the world's bestselling book. But whoever has time to read it all from cover to cover? Now here's a way of getting to know the Bible without having to read every chapter and verse.

No summary, no paraphrase, no commentary: just the Bible's own story in the Bible's own words.

'What an amazing concept! This compelling, concise, slimmed-down Scripture is a must for anyone who finds those sixty-six books a tad daunting.'
Paul Kerensa, comedian and script writer

'A great introduction to the main stories in the Bible and it helps you to see how they fit together. It would be great to give as a gift.'
Five-star review on Amazon

The One Hour Bible
978 0 281 07964 3 • £4.99

 spck.org.uk   /SPCKPublishing    @SPCKPublishing   @SPCK_Publishing